D0435726

# How To Benefit From

## STRESS

**BY**

**NICOLA M. TAURASO, M.D., F.A.A.P., F.R.S.H.**
Founder and Director
The GOTACH Center for Health
Frederick, Maryland

in collaboration with

**REV. L. RICHARD BATZLER, PH.D.**
Pastor, Faith United Church of Christ
Frederick, Maryland

*To Evelyn*  *a first and not a last*

**HVP**

Hidden Valley Press
7051 Poole Jones Road
Frederick, Maryland 21701

# HOW TO BENEFIT FROM STRESS

All inquiries should be addressed to
Hidden Valley Press,
7051 Poole Jones Road,
Frederick, Maryland 21701

First Printing, 1979

Printed in USA

Library of Congress Catalog Number: 79—003843

ISBN: 0—935710—00—0

# DEDICATION

To George Ann Mudge whose undaunting faith
has inspired me to move into the frontiers of holistic health and to my mother whose faith and encouragement instilled a desire within me to pursue
new frontiers.

# TABLE OF CONTENTS

# ACKNOWLEDGMENTS

How do I acknowledge the contributions of so many individuals? Writing a book is not an independent event. It is rather the result of the accumulated efforts of the many who have influenced my thinking.

I would not be where I am today were it not for the forceful guidance of my parents. My mother's faith in me never faltered. I credit her for the influence she had upon the development of the sensitive aspect of my ego. My father, the inveterate philosopher, had the ability of distilling a complex situation to the essential ingredients. I am still learning from him even after his physical death.

Of my teachers I am moved to acknowledge two groups. The Xavierian Brothers, who expected only excellence during prep school, taught me that there was an obligation to strive toward one's full potential. Anything less was just not acceptable. It was during the junior year of prep school that I developed the burning desire to explore the relationship between the body and mind — a desire which was nurtured for almost thirty years before it became manifested. The Jesuits of Boston College helped to refine my thinking and taught me logic. Although I now believe that relying solely on logic can interfere with one's mental growth and development, the inquiring approach taught by the Jesuits was stimulating.

Of my mentors I single out five individuals. The Reverends Michael P. Walsh, S.J., and George F. Lawlor, S.J., both of Boston College, guided me into medical school, where I was to receive the basic training of a physician. Dr. Louis Dienes of Harvard Medical School introduced me to the sensitivity and love of all of God's creatures. Dr. John F. Enders, also of Harvard Medical School, taught me the scientific method and how to perform research. His instruction and guidance helped to further refine my abilities to investigate the workings behind the law of nature. Dr. Alexis Shelokov, my mentor at the National Institutes of Health, was both a teacher and a second father. He had a profound influence upon both my professional and personal growth and development. We spent many hours chatting about the interrelating influence of body, mind, and spirit, long before the word "holistic" was being applied to health.

A very particular thanks to Filomena C. Morton, my sister. In May 1976 when I was plagued with cluster migraine headaches (and my fellow physicians were unable to help me), it was Fil who suggested I begin to assume the responsibility for my own illness and learn how to cure myself. I traveled to San Diego and accomplished both feats. This was my introduction to the concept and reality of holistic health. I also thank Fil for her fearless and painstaking efforts in critically reviewing the manuscript and for suggesting the title of the book.

Special thanks to George Ann Mudge who shares the dedication of this book with my mother. Her undaunting faith inspired me to move into the frontiers of holistic health. Additionally, her patience, support, encouragement, and assistance were ever present during the actual writing of this book.

I acknowledge the inspiration and help of Rev. L. Richard Batzler, Ph.D., who has been more than just a collaborator in **all** phases of this work. He is a friend who is most sensitive to the workings of both the spirit within us and Christ. His contribution of Chapter 15 (Spiritual Health and Stress) reflects his commitment and sensitivity to the Word.

John Shumacher contributed the section on Yoga and J. Frederick Tresselt discusses Aikido in Chapter 12 (Benefits of the Meditative Exercises). Both John and Fred are deeply committed to their respective disciplines and I have learned much from both of them.

I am also grateful to Fay W. Joy for her preparation and donation of the artwork within the text, for the painstaking efforts of Cyrie Barnes who assisted in editing, and to Sue Battistone for her dedication and efforts (beyond the usual call of duty) in typing all phases of the manuscript.

Lastly I acknowledge the contributions of my patients and all those who look to me for guidance and advice. If they only knew how much I am learning from them! I sincerely feel that, as long as I am open to listening to and learning from them, I am on the correct path.

Quotation from "The Dimension of Wellness: the Holistic Viewpoint" by Richard H. Svihus, M.D., *American Holistic Medicine,*

Volume 1, number 1, p. 20, February, 1979. Reprinted by permission of the author.

Quotation from "Coping With Stress," the sixteenth in a series of essays by Robert R. Leichtman, M.D. and Carl Japikse on *The Art of Living*. Copyright 1978 by Ariel Press, 2582 Shrewsbury Road, Columbus, Ohio 43221. Reprinted by permission of the senior author.

Quotation from *Zen Macrobiotic Cooking* by Michel Abehsera. Copyright 1968 by Michel Abehsera. Published by Avon Books, a division of The Hearst Corporation, 959 Eighth Avenue, New York, New York 10019. Reprinted by permission of the author.

Quotation from *Sugar Blues* by William Dufty. Copyright 1975 by William Dufty. Published by Warner Books, Inc., 75 Rockefeller Plaza, New York, N.Y. 10019. Reprinted by permission of the author.

Quotation from *Dietary Goals for the United States,* by the Select Committee on Nutrition and Human Needs of the United States Senate, 1977. Printed by the U.S. Government Printing Office. A public document.

# FOREWORD

It is now well recognized that the major cause of illness is the total stress in the individual: chemical, physical, mental, emotional, and spiritual. This book is an attempt to present and describe in common every day language some **practical** suggestions for incorporating the concepts of an holistic approach to daily living.

One of the aims of holistic health is to form a partnership between the health professional and the individual seeking help. Holistic medical practitioners view their patients as therapeutic partners and teach self-responsibility, in which each individual becomes an active, knowledgeable participant in the achievement and maintenance of his or her optimum level of health. The authors have tried to keep this focus in presenting the information and in describing a concept of using stress as a growth and development experience. Merely coping with stress is not enough. Our aim is to present an approach by which the individual can learn to benefit from actual or potential stress situations.

Although overt stress situations are easily identified, latent unrecognized stress can also be a source of many difficulties in one's personal, vocational, and social life. We hope that this book will teach you not only how to recognize this latent stress, but also, more importantly, **how** to deal with and even **benefit** from it.

If the reader is expecting either a magic formula which will work by mere invocation or some spirit to materialize "out of the blue," touch his magic wand, and say that everything is all-right, then read no further. The approach to benefiting from stress described in this book will work provided the individual is sincere and is willing to do his share. "Faith without works is dead" is as true today as it has been from time immemorial.

A beautiful and fascinating element of nature is that the human is endowed with fantastic recuperative and regenerative abilities.

Also, we have been given power over ourselves. Individuals who are willing to assume self-responsibility for their physical, mental, emotional and spiritual health will find the journey not only worthwhile but also exciting.

So let us move along together and experience the fullness of life, holistically.

Nicola M. Tauraso

# CHAPTER 1

# THE CHALLENGE

I am reminded of the great advice given to me by those superior teachers, the Jesuit priests of Boston College, that, before discussing a point or subject, one should begin by defining the terms or subject matter.

Of course, this sounds reasonable. However, all too often this important factor is neglected, thereby resulting in confusion. For example, if we were to describe the characteristics of a piece of fruit, it would be important that we specify the fruit or else one might visualize fruit other than that which we set out to describe. And so it applies to our subject matter.

## What is stress?

At the outset, it is important to establish both a definition and an attitude about stress. Out there in the so-called real (objective) world there is no such thing as stress! At least, stress does not exist in the same way as an automobile, a banana or a dog. If I were to show a banana to 100 individuals, all would agree that the banana was indeed a banana. So it would be with most things that exist in the physical world.

There are no objective criteria defining stress. Then what is stress? The basic initial definition I am proposing is that *"stress is a condition within man of tension and upheaval brought about by man's reaction to an internal or external situation."*

Stress can be viewed as a positive and good force in our lives. This may be difficult for individuals who have been taught to avoid stressful conditions to accept. I hope that at the conclusion of this book, you will be convinced of the positive nature and value of stress, so that you go on and truly enjoy the rest of your life.

## The internal and external sources of stress

There can be internal and external stressful physical conditions. It's a hot summer day. We're not drinking enough fluids. Consequently, a stressful state of affairs ensues causing our thirst center to ask for more fluids. If we then drink adequate liquids, our thirst is satisfied and the stressful situation alleviated.

What would have happened if we had not had a thirst alarm reaction or if we had not responded once the thirst warning sounded? We would have become increasingly dehydrated, our salt concentration could have decreased to abnormally low levels, and eventually we could have experienced sunstroke and died. Knowing this, we can easily conclude that the thirst alarm reaction responding to a particular stress was not only good but necessary for survival.

We break a leg, causing another stressful condition within our body. Although the orthopedic surgeon sets the leg so it will heal straight, it is the body's innate programmed intelligence which very naturally and normally initiates the machinery to begin the healing process. We accept and take for granted these types of physical stresses.

There can also be mental, emotional and spiritual stressful conditions within man. Since man is not a simple being, since he is a complex being having body, mind, emotions and spirit, stressful conditions are almost never simple: never purely physical without mental, emotional and spiritual overtones; never purely mental without physical, emotional and spiritual overtones; rarely purely emotional without physical, mental and spiritual overtones.

Many physical dis-eases result from man's negative attitude to mental, emotional and/or spiritual stresses. The physical condition is a mere reflection of the individual's mental and spiritual health. Unless a genuine cure occurs at the basic mental, emotional, and spiritual level, the physical dis-ease progresses.

Factors outside of us become stressful when we make them so. Unlike the apple, which will be an apple to all men, a situation may be stressful to one person, a challenge to another, or a welcome form of recreation to yet another.

I love horseback riding. I thoroughly enjoy this form of recreation and sport. I know some individuals who, if you were to put them on the back of the most gentle horse, would consider this one of the worst forms of physical, mental, and emotional torture.

I see children in my office all day long. To some I'm a friend they enjoy seeing and playing with. They enjoy the relationship of my playing doctor and their playing patient. On the other hand, there are other children who come into my office and already they have worked themselves up into such an emotional tizzy that they are actually suffering.

The situation as it exists in the outside objective world is the same for both children, that is, a doctor in an office. However, within the minds of these two children are two totally different creations. In most cases, the type of reaction observed in children is a mere reflection of where one or both of the parents are mentally. More on this later.

Let us now add to the basic definition of stress given earlier: *"Stress is a condition **created within man by man himself** of tension and upheaval brought about by his reaction to an internal or external situation."* The bold portion has been added.

## Who is prone to stress?

Are there some individuals more prone to have difficulty coping with stress? In my opinion, there are. Then, what makes them that way? I believe it is their childhood programming.

When we were born our bio-computer memory bank, our brain, was devoid of information and programming. As we grew up, bits of information from our sensing experience (e.g., sight, hearing, smell, taste and touch) were filed away in our memory. We drew from this bank of information throughout our lives to develop responses to new situations as they arose. These new experiences were also stored, and our subconscious continued to draw from the totality of our past experiences to form our behavior.

The reason why our very early childhood experiences were so important is because these formed the foundation upon which our basic personality was constructed. During our early childhood we acted automatically without giving conscious thought to our actions. We didn't have the maturity to know what we were doing. What was happening was that our subconscious was developing and acting as an independent entity outside our conscious control.

By the time we became adults, the subconscious was well on its way to assuming tremendous control over our mental processes and our emotional responses. After we grew up and matured, some of us may have wondered why we did this or that. If we didn't like the way we reacted, we may have attempted to change. Anyone who has tried to change a habit of response knows how must energy it takes to change.

Unfortunately, many individuals are completely ruled by their subconscious and remain victims of their inner subconscious self until they free themselves from this prison.

It would have been ideal for our parents to have appreciated the significance of their every action while we were infants and children. But, lacking the ideal, we are now challenged to do something to recapture what is rightfully ours. Our conscious mind-self must rule over our untrained subconscious.

Let us consider some of the inner sources of stress, some of our behavior patterns which cause our lives to be stressful.

• **FEAR** is probably the most powerful of the negative emotions. Most of the other negative emotions have their basis in fear. Fear is usually a conditioned reaction to some early unpleasant event which is being projected to some present or future situation. Morbid fears can cause serious mental, emotional and physical dis-ease states and must be controlled.

• **ANGER** is a self-destructive negative emotion. When a person is emotionally immature he is apt to give way to outbursts of anger. Expressing anger accomplishes nothing, other than bringing the wrath of others down upon you. It also dissipates your energy. Other negative emotions, such as hatred, jealousy, sorrow, anxiety, envy, and crying spells dissipate your mental strength, cause tension-fatigue and are self-destructive.

• **IMPATIENCE** causes you to be less tolerant of others. You judge others by your own high standards and when they do not perform as quickly or as well as you expect, you frequently stew inside and lack peace.

• **RIGIDITY** or inflexibility places tremendous burdens upon your inner self. Rigid people nearly always seem to be looking for something to be upset about.

• **PERFECTIONISM** is a form of rigidity. Since you don't have a crystal ball, since you do not have access to the Master's grand plan, do you really know what the absolute perfect is? Consequently, perfectionists are almost always disappointed, if not of others, surely of themselves when they think they have made a mistake.

• **INABILITY TO RELAX,** always on the go, leads you to become exhausted. Constant pushing leads to stress.

• **EXCESSIVE COMPETITION** adds pressures that will ultimately result in stress to you, your family, friends and co-workers.

• **LACK OF HUMOR AND ENTHUSIASM** is a kind of sour attitude that breeds stress. A humorless person is generally one who is seething inside and full of self-reproach and self-contempt.

• **CHRONIC WORRYING** is a symptom of insecurity and it reflects a lack of self-confidence. It is a bad habit which can destroy your health because it causes nervous fatigue.

• **MENTAL DEPRESSION** is the end result of frequent unhappy moods and losing hope. Mental depression can be a very vicious negative emotion because it can lead to utter despair. Your recuperative strength is sapped to the point where it becomes very difficult to recover. It may become a bad habit that requires much energy to turn around, energy that you don't have.

This short list of some of the inner sources of stress should serve as a stimulus for you to examine your own personality for possible sources of inner turmoil. The destructive nature of stress is further described in Chapter 5.

Some individuals are more prone to the negative aspects of stress. They essentially become victims of a way of thinking and behaving. But all is not lost.

## Is there any hope?

Of course there is! As mentioned earlier, we are endowed with fantastic recuperative and regenerative abilities. All we need to do is to assume the responsibility for being where we are, to have an open mind and recognize that we are causing the negative conditions arising in our life, and finally, to *"grab the bull by the horns"* and make the necessary changes in our way of thinking and acting, so that we can live and enjoy life to the fullest, as the Creator has always intended.

# CHAPTER 2

# HOW WE GOT TO WHERE WE ARE

## The mind/brain as a sophisticated biocomputer and the psychodynamics of our early childhood programming

Let us consider for a moment that our brain functions as a sophisticated biocomputer and that the abstract entity we call our mind functions through this biocomputer in a way which is unique to each individual.

Psychiatrists and psychologists are now appreciating the fact that the mind/brain complex is a biocomputer more intricate than computers made by man. Our biocomputer not only has memory of past events, but it also has the ability to synthesize and make its own programming, the so called software of man-made computers. Even more fascinating is that our biocomputer has emotions and a free will, unlike the machines made by man. I realize this might be a shock to the creators of Star Wars, Wonder Woman, the Six Million Dollar Man, etc. who may think that they have duped us into believing that man-made computer machines can have free will and emotions!

Research is demonstrating that man's biocomputer is complex and has thought-creative ability. If we are to begin to understand ourselves, we need to know how it functions.

In the beginning when we were born we had no ideas because we had no experiences upon which to build. I will not quarrel with those who believe in reincarnation and karma, or those who firmly believe our life is predestined from birth. I believe that the evolution of the journey our soul is now taking can be influenced by our free will and our thinking.

At one time in medical school we were taught that an infant could not see until he was about 4-6 weeks of age. We now know this is not true. Infants see as soon as they are born, but they do not know what they are seeing.

At about 4 weeks of age they begin to associate a human face with gratifying experiences such as fondling, food and drink to satisfy their hunger, and a dry diaper change to relieve a wet, cold, and messy feeling. They begin to use their eyes to follow their mother (or their fathers in some households!) who interprets this as the baby seeing and recognizing her.

One of the most common questions mothers used to ask was: Does my baby see yet? Can my baby see now? Mothers don't ask these questions today. Many are becoming aware of the fact that babies see as soon as they are born and are now requesting that doctors delay instilling into the eyes medicine required to prevent gonococcal infection, a condition which used to be one of the greatest causes of total blindness. Mothers are now concerned that instilling silver nitrate or antibiotic drops causes irritation and interferes with early bonding between mother and infant. In my opinion, too much is being made of this by physicians and parents who may want to believe that a simple event in one's life has such drastic consequences. *It is the accumulation of negative events and, more importantly, how we are taught to deal with them that determines our ultimate behavior and coping ability.*

The infant who is beginning to employ his eyes to follow his mother is beginning to draw simple interpretive conclusions from life's experiences. As more bits of information get stored in this biocomputer, the interpretive conclusions become increasingly complex and manifest in our daily lives as actions and reactions.

Sometimes we recognize the reasons behind our actions. Most of the time, however, we act quickly and spontaneously, and the reasons behind our actions are hidden in the deeper recesses of our subconscious mind.

We indeed have two minds: conscious and subconscious. Our conscious mind functions only while we are awake and aware. It is concerned with our free-will decisions and actions. The subconscious mind functions 24 hours a day while we are awake and while we are in the deeper levels of sleep. It controls the automatic functions of our body, such as heart rate, breathing, blood pressure, digestion, etc. In addition, our habits and automatic habit responses such as smoking, overeating, anger, fear, anxiety, love, tolerance, etc. are mostly powered by our subconscious mind. More about this in Chapter 7.

One school of modern psychiatry and psychology teaches that we would benefit by going into our past and finding the reasons why we act the way we do. Supposedly, with this knowledge we can begin to understand the reasons behind our actions. Hopefully, we may then be able to change those patterned programmed responses which are stumbling blocks on our path toward growth and understanding.

It is important for us to recognize that the reasons for our actions today are deeply rooted in our past experiences, especially those of our childhood. We believe, however, that spending too much time conjuring negative past experiences may actually be harmful. By so doing we reemphasize the thoughts we wish to change.

What difference does it really make that our negative outlook on life may have been due to possibly an unloving mother, an overly stern father, or even a very cruel aunt? Is it really beneficial to know that we can relate a particular negative personality trait to some specific traumatic event, such as the rejection of a lover, a divorce, the loss of a family member, etc.? Does knowing the cause justify our continued negative behavior? The answers to all of these questions is an unqualified "no."

We are indeed victims of our childhood programming. Essentially we act the way we do because we saw our mothers and fathers act similarly when they were faced with challenges. It was the people around us during our early formative years who provided the "software" programming for our mental biocomputer.

Granted there are individual variations in our response patterns that make us unique. We all do have different imaginations through which we create a reaction response that is ours and no one elses. We may all have perfect 20/20 vision as we view a particular event. However, we may each interpret what we see completely differently.

I am reminded of the time when I was sitting in my living room reading and I couldn't help being distracted by my 3 young children who were experiencing difficulty in their play situation. Within minutes this had escalated to all-out-war! They all came to me crying, pointing an accusing finger at each other, never at themselves. I asked them to calm down. I then listened to each version of the story. Not only did I hear 3 different descriptions of the event, but, most importantly, none of them coincided with what I thought I saw! They were so different that, had I not seen with my own eyes, I would never have known that they were describing the same event I had just witnessed.

The children were sincere in their recollection of the experience. I was convinced that they were not lying. They were actually telling the truth as they perceived it.

Each child asked to have the other punished. I was unable to decide who was right, who was wrong. I instructed all three to go to one of their bedrooms and to resolve their differences peacefully. If they were unable to do this, I would step in and punish them all. Five minutes later, since I hadn't heard from them, I peeked into the bedroom. All three were having a delightful time playing a game, completely oblivious to what apparently had gone on before! I did not realize at the time what I had done, which was to ask them to assume responsibility for their actions. There was a small incentive thrown into the instructions, the threat of punishment had they not succeeded. They met the challenge nobly, considering they were 5, 6, and 7 year olds!

Let us appreciate the fact that we are what we are and act the way we do because of our childhood programming. Let us not stop here and cop out. We don't have to be victims of our past. We don't have to be imprisoned by a negative subconscious. If we believe we are truly spiritual beings undergoing a human experience, our potential then is infinite!

## CHAPTER 3

# WHERE DO WE GO FROM HERE?

I sincerely hope that, after reading this book, you will be convinced that you do have all the ingredients within yourself, that you have all the power within you, and that you can mobilize this inner strength to handle any challenge.

First, develop the positive attitude that you **can** achieve what you hope to achieve and then some.

This book describes three basic techniques which can be used both in developing a positive mental attitude and in dealing constructively with stress, namely, *affirmation, meditation, and guided imagery.* These are described in more detail in Chapters 16 and 17.

In the meantime, we are going to begin to use the techniques of *affirmation* to establish a positive belief system within ourselves. Set aside a short amount of time each day for affirmation. Begin in the morning after you have awakened and possibly while you're washing your face, combing your hair or shaving. Your affirmations will be enhanced if you state them to yourself while looking in a mirror. By doing this first thing in the morning, you can get yourself *psyched up* to be who and what you want to be. Repeat your affirmations upon retiring at night. This will set your mind with images which your subconscious will turn over and over while you sleep.

If you have a particular negative problem or challenge, write it out, state it to yourself **once**, tear the paper up, and go through the ritual of throwing it away. **Never repeat that statement again to yourself nor to anyone else!** What you're doing here is recognizing the fact that there exists a challenge within you. This serves as a reference point of identification in your mental biocomputer. The reason why the negative statement should not be repeated is because you do not wish to add psychic energy to a situation you wish to change or eliminate. If you repeat to yourself that "I am sick" or "I am tired," you are perpetuating a picture within your

11

mind of the very condition you do not want. Be careful about language.
Let us begin with a three part affirmation:

I HAVE DIFFICULTY COPING WITH STRESS AND THE EVERY DAY CHALLENGES OF LIFE.

I DON'T WANT TO HAVE DIFFICULTY COPING WITH STRESS AND THE EVERY DAY CHALLENGES OF LIFE.

**I HAVE THE POWER WITHIN ME TO HANDLE ANY CHALLENGE COMING MY WAY.** (Repeat).

State the first and second statement only once, repeat the third three times and as often as you wish to impress that belief upon your mind.

## What is our goal?

Before we are able to achieve a goal, we must first have one. Many individuals aren't moving anywhere in life because they have not mapped out any destination. They are just aimlessly wandering, confused about what to do. That's OK. But, don't complain when you're standing still and going nowhere as the rest of the world passes by you.

I have known a few individuals who appeared to be quite satisfied doing nothing with their lives. However, most are not this way. Man is endowed with a spirit that yearns for fulfillment and meaning. Our spirit ever seeks to grow, mature, and evolve to higher levels of consciousness. The average individual has that innate desire to leave his mark upon the world. When he feels that he is not accomplishing this, he is discontent and restless. This often leads to depression and dispair.

Few of us have been taught how to set goals. If we have, we were probably not told how to achieve them. At times in our lives, especially during times of stress, we do set goals and surprise ourselves by our achievement. Observe what happens to a nation of people when a stressful challenge comes along. They unite for a common purpose, frequently for survival. They determine their goals. They pool their energies and move forward in a straight line, not in circles, toward their goal.

You are composed of a body, mind and spirit. Determine what you want to accomplish in life. Unite the three aspects of your being. Use your energy from the billions of cells within your body, from your mind, and your spirit to move toward your goal. You will be surprised at what you can accomplish. You will be satisfied. You will like yourself because you are in control.

Think out your goals and put them in writing. Modify them as you go along and as your needs and desires change. Be specific about what you desire. Determine what you want to achieve in your personal life, your job, your social life and most importantly your spiritual life.

Consideration of your personal life might include thinking about your desires for fulfillment of your inner self, your family (spouse, children, mother, father, brothers, sisters and relatives), and your friends. Allow others the freedom you expect to express their free will according to their creative imagination, that is, "Do unto others as you would want others to do unto you."

Establish relationships that are not addictive. Don't expect to own other individuals, not even your children. Help others who need your guidance in such a way that encourages them to develop their own individuality and independence from you. At the same time you must be careful not to become dependent upon them.

Establish priorities with your goals, such as God, yourself, family, friends, job and social life. As you develop an holistic attitude about God, you will begin to experience unification of your body, mind, emotions and spirit. Relationship with your family, friends, job and social life will improve. Developing an awareness of each of these entities in your life will prepare you and lead you into an awareness and appreciation of others. Christ did say: "Put your house in order." When you do, you will experience that everyone else's house is in order.

Consideration of your job might include whether you are in a job which best suits your talents and interests. You will, of course, be much happier if your work and play are the same, if you are doing something you do well, and if your work challenges your creative imaginative self. If you set your goals for money and material things, you are again developing an addictive relationship. As with all such relationships, there is a price you must pay. Be aware of the costs in terms of emotional drain, possible boredom, lack of creative fulfillment, interference with personal life development, etc. If you're willing to pay the price, then proceed as you desire. Let us always remember that each of us has the free will to choose our goals and the paths we wish to take to attain them.

Do not be afraid to change jobs in midstream even when at times your security is challenged. Later, you will discover that challenges are placed before us for the purposes of growth and development. When we shy away from a challenge, we stunt our expansion in that direction. Maybe you're in a dead end job and another promotion may further entrench you in that dead end one way road to nowhere. Chapter 8 describes in more detail how to use your challenges for growth and development.

Consider the goals in your social life. Again, establish priorities as to what is important to you in your development. In many aspects of your social life, the problem of addiction and misplaced priorities can be overwhelming. You may find yourself caught up in an ever increasing vicious circle of friends whose energies are negative and misdirected. Since you are affected by the mental (thought) energies of others, you begin to think like those around you, and you may begin to experience their mental, spiritual, and even physical aberrations and dis-eases. Napoleon Hill in his book, *Think And Grow Rich,* advises to be careful of the company you keep because you will become like the company you keep. Amazing! My father, who never went beyond the first grade in Italy, told me the same thing as a child. It took many sad experiences before I realized that my father, Napoleon Hill, and others were stating a Universal Law. Scientists are now discovering in the laboratory that thoughts are real, they are forms of energy, that we have a mental energy field around ourselves, and that we not only affect the thoughts of people around us, but we are also affected and influenced by their thoughts and feelings.

Probably the most important goals to establish in our life are those concerning our spiritual development. Let us be aware of the spirit within, establish contact with it, dialogue with it, and discover the needs and directions for our lives. We may want to ask ourselves those three most famous questions: *Who am I? What am I? Where am I going?* If you are sincere about it, answers will come.

It is important to establish contact with our Creator, our God, whose infinite life Force flows through us all. This enables us to be energized at times when it may appear that maybe we're losing ground.

We ask individuals taking our Coping With Stress seminars who may be atheists or agnostics to play a game for a few weeks and just pretend that there is an Infinite Intelligent Force who is responsible for all that we see around us in the Universe. We ask them to meditate upon this Creative Intelligence and just keep their minds open for an experience.

What happens was described by a professed agnostic after completing one of our seminars. He told me that, at first, he considered "all that stuff about the spirit" which we talked about during our first session to be "a lot of hogwash" but that he decided to play the game as we had asked him to do. "You know," he said, "as I meditated more, I began to ask myself those very dangerous questions, 'Who am I?, What am I?, Where am I going?'. You know, there is something out there bigger than all of us!"

My reply was: "There is? Keep on searching. You're on the right track."

I shall always remember not only his words, but also the expression on his face. It was similar to that of a child on his first visit to a real live circus: eyes wide open, a glowing face reflecting a reawakening of the inner spirit. Bob allowed himself to be receptive to God's infinite intelligence and power. He became a channel through which the Creative Intelligent Force flowed. Bob overcame the stressful challenges which prompted him to take the seminar, and opportunities immediately opened up in both his vocational and social life.

## Can we reach our goal?

Of course we can.

From this day forward we are not going to look backwards at our past, except on occasion when we wish to recognize the fact that there exists a negative situation which we wish to change. After we recognize the existence of a particular negative situation, let us decide what positive condition we wish to create. Then give all our energy to the positive condition so that we can attract it to our consciousness.

From this day forward we are not going to make excuses for our mistakes. We are not going to blame our husbands or our wives or our children or our bosses or anyone else for our errors. We are going to stand up in front of a mirror if we have to, and affirm:

**I AM RESPONSIBLE FOR MY ACTIONS! I AM RESPONSIBLE NOT ONLY FOR THE GOOD BUT ALSO FOR THE BAD THAT HAPPENS TO ME.**

**I AM THE MASTER OF MY FATE AND MY LIFE IS WHAT I MAKE IT.**

**I AM MASTER OF MY FATE AND CAPTAIN OF MY SOUL.**

In summary, go within to your inner spirit, determine what your real goals in life should be, set your sails, and direct your ship in an undeviating course toward your goal. Always maintain faith in your God-given spiritual power for the strength to persevere. **Your total holistic evolvement is just an attitude away.**

# CHAPTER 4

# HOW TO ACHIEVE OUR GOAL

## The Holistic Approach

Our approach to coping with stress encompasses the prinicples of holism. The derivation of the word and concept of holism was very well described by Dr. Richard H. Svihus in a paper entitled "The Dimensions of Wellness: The Holistic Viewpoint," delivered at the founding meeting of the American Holistic Medical Association, Denver, Colorado, May, 1978 and published in *American Holistic Medicine,* volume 1, pages 19 to 25, February, 1979. Quoting from Dr. Svihus:

*The words "holistic" and "holism" first appear to have been used by Jan Smuts in his book, **Holism and Evolution**, published in 1926. Jan Smuts served as a general in the British army and as prime minister of South Africa. In his book, he describes an evolutionary concept in which "Holism underlies the synthetic tendency in the universe." Entities growing, developing, and evolving become at some point complete in their nature, so that their wholeness becomes greater than the mere sum of their parts. They then move to new levels of being – new "wholes" – brought about by the creative force within, which he calls holism.*

*The whole-making tendency in evolution, according to Smuts, is nothing but the gradual development and stratification of a progressive series of wholes, stretching from the inorganic beginnings to the highest levels of spiritual creation.*

*Wholeness, healing, holiness – all expressions and ideas springing from the same root in language as in experience – lie on the rugged upward path of the universe."*

If you acknowledge the fact that we have a triune nature of body, mind and spirit, then we are total individuals only when our body-self, mind-self, and spirit-self are unified to work in harmony with each other.

All too often individuals are dis-coordinated. Their body, mind, and spirit parts function as separate schizophrenic entities working against each other.

Holistic means to be *holy,* to function as a whole *I*.

Figure 4-1 depicts *The Holy Trinity of Holistic Health,* that is body, mind and spirit. To achieve total holistic health, we are first to consider nutrition and physical exercise as partners in establishing and maintaining a healthy body. Second, develop mental exercise programs to help us achieve self-mastery and self-regulation. And, third, breathe life into our spirit by creating a positive healthy belief factor and developing a capacity both to give and to receive love.

The Holy Trinity of Holistic Health

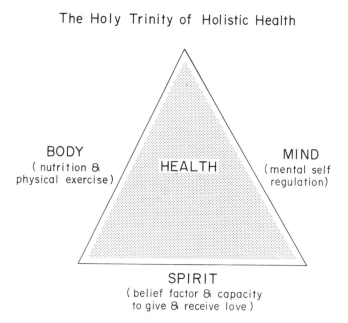

Figure 4-1

Figure 4-2 shows the *Factors Influencing Physical Health,* namely nutrition, exercise and rest. It is important to nourish our bodies with foods nature has intended humans to consume. Much of the food we consume has been grown in fields saturated with chemical fertilizers. Insecticides, pesticides and herbicides, designed to kill insects, pests and unwanted weeds, are added. These poisons get into the very foods we consume. Although government scientists, in their finite and limited wisdom, establish so-called *safe* limits for these poisons, has it ever occurred to them that these are man-made chemicals mostly derived from crude oil? Has it ever occurred to them that nature never intended that these chemicals find their way into our food chain, and perhaps the *safe* limit is zero? It is not surprising to discover that many of these chemicals are now being found to cause cancer in animals; more are being found daily. It should not be surprising to realize that the incidence of cancer and degenerative diseases is increasing as we are consuming more and more chemically altered foods.

Much of the food we purchase in the supermarket is chemically altered or has contained within it chemical additives, such as preservatives, sweeteners, coloring, etc. We are indeed paying the price for consuming a diet which is contrary to nature's intention (Chapter 10).

## Factors Influencing Physical Health

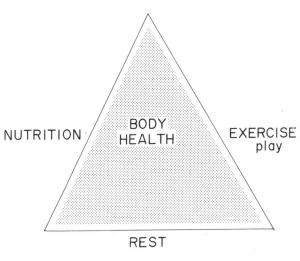

Figure 4-2

Another aspect of body health is exercise. Our exercise should be a form of play, not work. If we perform our calisthenics in the morning, constantly looking at the clock eager to get it all over with, that exercise program will be harmful to our health. As with work, an effective exercise program should be our play (Chapter 11).

Rest is important for regeneration of our physical energy. The human body does have fantastic recuperative and regenerative abilities. Unlike our automobile that needs to have a carburator or fuel pump replaced when something goes wrong, the human body has an innate intelligence programmed to repair, regenerate and in certain cases replace dis-eased tissues and organs. The body must be healthy to accomplish these feats, and rest is a necessary requirement.

Figure 4-3 lists the *Keys to Mental Self-Regulation:* imagination, visualization and belief-factor to achieve mind power. Let us learn to use our imagination in a positive and constructive manner, rather than in a negative self-defeating way.

It is important to develop our powers of visualization. Scientists in the field of mind science are discovering that achieving goals is directly related to how well we are able to create visual pictures in our minds. You can be taught how to develop your powers of visualization (Chapter 7).

An indispensible part of your mind power depends upon your belief factor. It is the power behind your thoughts. You may have a creative imagination and an excellent power to visualize, but if you don't believe, all will be in vain. I have known individuals who were not very positive in their imagination and couldn't visualize very well, but they had a belief in something and their powerful belief pulled them through. On the other hand, your strong powers of belief may work against you if your imagination and what you visu-

Keys to Mental Self – Regulation

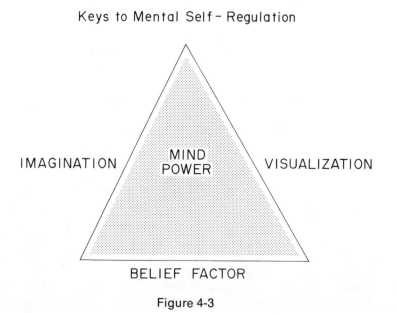

Figure 4-3

alize are negative. Belief is a two edged sword. It can be positive or negative (Chapter 7).

Figure 4-4 describes the *Factors Influencing Spiritual Health:* love understanding and tolerance, and belief factor. We must truly learn how to love, how to give and to receive love, how to be a channel through which God's infinite love flows into, through and around us for ourselves and others. Hate and the other negative emotions dissipate your energy and block you from achieving the wellness state. If you have a serious dis-ease, it will be difficult to cure yourself if you go to bed hating half the people you met that day.

Understanding and tolerance are important. These are outward expressions of your love and concern for both yourself and your fellow man. The mind is convinced by outward expressions of genuine concern. Start by being understanding and tolerant of yourself. Frequently, an individual is his own worst enemy. He may be full of self-hate, self-pity, and self-reproach. This negative energy becomes a frontal assault against himself. He will suffer the consequences of this self-destructive behavior. Develop a tolerance of yourself, then shower your good fortune upon others (Chapters 15 and 18).

### Factors Influencing Spiritual Health

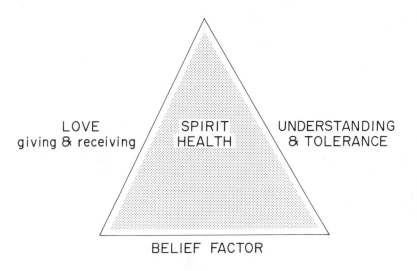

LOVE
giving & receiving

SPIRIT
HEALTH

UNDERSTANDING
& TOLERANCE

BELIEF  FACTOR

Figure 4-4

The belief factor depicted in Figure 4-4 is different from that described earlier (Fig. 4-3). We are now referring to one's belief in a

Superior Being, God. It has been demonstrated over and over throughout the history of man that belief and faith in the power of God heals. If for no other reason than to be practical, let us develop a positive attitude and belief about a Superior Being, who is everywhere (omnipresent), all-knowing (omniscient) and all-powerful (omnipotent). As we develop our affirmations and belief systems and as we progress and follow this advice, we shall experience the healing power of God.

Edgar Cayce, the well-known psychic healer, sometimes referred to as the sleeping prophet, believed that the spirit is life, the mind the builder, and the physical the effect (Figure 4-5). What we see and experience as physical dis-eases and states of physical wellness are what the mind creates as a result of either a sick or a well spirit. In my medical school training, we were never taught to view dis-ease in this way. But, as I do now and have for several years, all of what used to be enigmas because of my previous way of thinking now make sense. I had eyes but I did not see. Now that my spirit is beginning to awaken, I am seeing, and it is making sense.

True healing is definitely an adventure in consciousness. As we observe individuals who experience spontaneous miraculous cures from dis-eases such as cancer, we also observe a change in their level of consciousness. More about this later.

Cayce's Concept of Wellness / Dis-ease

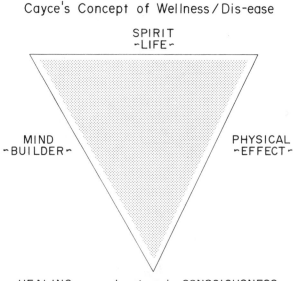

HEALING – an adventure in CONSCIOUSNESS

Figure 4-5

*Factors Influencing Coping Ability* include the emotions, environment and constitution (Figure 4-6).

The negative emotions of fear, anger, hatred, guilt, and depression drain our energy. Energy is what keeps our physical body, mind and emotions intact. Dissipate energy and eventually something is going to give. Fear is the most powerful of the negative emotions from which most of the others are derived.

Love is the most powerful of the positive emotions and can do more to energize the body, mind, emotions and spirit than any single factor. Learn to exercise it. Learn to be a lover!

We can recognize environmental sources of stress, such as social, nutritional, chemical, traumatic and illness. Some of these have already been discussed and others will be described later. We should consider these potential sources of environmental stress in our overall program of establishing an attitude about using stress as a useful encounter for growth.

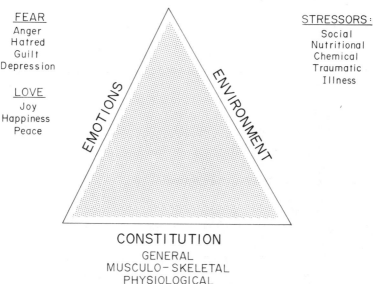

Factors Influencing Coping Ability

FEAR
Anger
Hatred
Guilt
Depression

LOVE
Joy
Happiness
Peace

STRESSORS:
Social
Nutritional
Chemical
Traumatic
Illness

EMOTIONS

ENVIRONMENT

CONSTITUTION
GENERAL
MUSCULO-SKELETAL
PHYSIOLOGICAL
GENETIC

Figure 4-6

Of course, your basic constitution may affect your coping ability. For instance, if you are a short man with a slight frame, it would probably not be prudent to get a job working on the docks with all those men weighing 200 plus pounds. You might be challenged beyond your physical powers if one of them ordered you to move a crate five times your size and weighing three times your weight! This should not discourage you because you may have it within your capabilities to be owner of the shipping concern and the boss of those physical giants. Take into consideration your general, musculo-skeletal, physiological, and genetic constitution as you move along in the discovery of yourself.

In this book, we present the holistic approach to daily living. We describe how you can keep your physical body in shape. We present information on nutrition and diet and emphasize the importance of good nutrition in keeping your physical body, and your mind well (Chapter 10). What we eat significantly affects the way we think, which, in turn, affects our ability to deal with potentially stressful situations.

We present information on how exercise affects your coping ability (Chapter 11).

We teach you how to handle environmental situations which affect your physical, mental and spiritual health (Chapter 8).

We offer alternative ways of dealing with emotional challenges. You **can** develop a positive attitude and watch your emotional conflicts resolve (Chapter 14).

We show how your spiritual development fits into this whole picture. You are taught how to go within and tap the source of your strength and you will experience spiritual growth as a result. (Chapters 7 and 15).

And lastly, we describe an approach to modifying life styles in ways which will foster a state of physical, mental, emotional, and spiritual wellness (Chapters 16, 17 and 18).

## Holistic health and medicine

The American Holistic Medical Association defines holistic health "as a state of well-being in which an individual's body, mind, emotions, and spirit are in tune with the natural, cosmic, and social environment."

Health is more than the absence of sickness. The healthy person enjoys robust vitality expressed as physical energy and strength, mental vigor, stable positive emotional responses and deeper spiritual motivation. This harmonious balance of body, mind and spirit is achievable.

A growing number of physicians and other health professionals now recognize the inseparability of mind, body and spirit in the encouragement of wellness and the prevention and treatment of illness.

Holistic medical practitioners view patients as therapeutic

partners and teach self-responsibility, in which each individual becomes an active knowledgeable participant in the achievement and maintenance of an optimum level of health. They treat the whole person, not just the condition. They recognize that health care means caring **about** as well as caring **for**, and that mental, emotional and environmental stress are often underlying components in physical illness.

Holistic medicine is a system of health care which emphasizes personal responsibility, and fosters a cooperative relationship among all those involved, leading toward optimal attunement of body, mind, emotions and spirit.

Holistic medical practitioners are not in opposition to customary medical methods. In fact, they seek to integrate traditional medicine with responsible, innovative approaches. Certain emerging alternative preventive and therapeutic methods are being shown by research to be sound, safe and effective.

Holistic medicine does encompass all safe modalities of diagnosis and treatment including drugs and surgery, but not to the exclusion of other approaches which accent patient responsibility. The holistic approach emphasizes the necessity of looking at the whole person, including analysis of physical, nutritional, environmental, emotional, spiritual and life style values.

Holistic health particularly focuses upon patient education and patient responsibility for personal efforts to achieve a harmonious balance of body, mind and spirit.

I have much hope in the American Holistic Medical Association, founded by a group of physicians under the leadership and direction of Dr. C. Norman Shealy, a man with a dream. The AHMA arose because of a need coming from the *grass roots* of our Country. Members of this organization are being challenged and, at times, persecuted by fellow physicians who refuse to accept new and changing concepts of health and dis-ease. The holistic approach is sound and sensible. This renaissance in attitude, which fosters self-awareness and self-responsibility about one's health, is going to revolutionize the application of medical care. The dedicated members of the AHMA have their work cut out for themselves to deliver what many are demanding. As the holistic movement spreads from individuals to groups, it is inevitable that more and more persons will benefit in body, mind and spirit.

**CHAPTER 5**

# STRESS AS
# A DESTRUCTIVE FORCE

As described in Chapter 1, *stress is a condition created within man by man himself of tension and upheaval brought about by his reaction to an internal or external situation.*

Let us now explore how and why stress becomes such a destructive force in many lives. Later we will learn how to use stress as a positive force in our growth, development and evolution.

## Nervous tension, the worry habit and chronic tiredness

Chronic tiredness is a way the body reacts negatively to stress and nervous tension. Let us look at some facts about stress and nervous tension to appreciate how this happens.

- Tension arises in people who are unable to cope with their fast paced life. These people tend to lead an unbalanced life and seem to have inadequate knowledge and wisdom about what it really takes to keep their body, mind and spirit healthy. They center their lives around unimportant things outside of themselves and when the outer world appears to be disintegrating, they become tense and uptight.

  First attempt to appreciate the fact that you can learn to completely overcome any degree of nervous tension you might have. Choose goals which have meaning and purpose to your inner self. Do not make any one material goal an addiction. Start with the top priority on your list keeping in mind a flexible attitude so that, as you become self-confident, the feeling to march forward gains momentum.

- Tiredness or fatigue seems to prevail in the lives of many. In some cases there appears to be a reasonable need for rest and sleep. However, when the body insists on resting for no apparent reason, then we have the option to look further within our being to correct the imbalance (e.g. inharmonious relationships, frustrating situations, inadequate diet, lack of exercise, etc.). In a way, tiredness is a protective device to force an individual to rest his body. Rest is one of the three factors influencing physical health. Rest and sleep are the usual ways the body cures itself of the normal degree of fatigue. During certain phases of rest and sleep the human brain cycles in *alpha* rhythm, the regenerative brain wave (Chapter 7).

Recreation is another way we use to counteract mental and physical fatigue. Diverting your mind from unpleasant work and turning it to play and laughter appears to have great therapeutic value.

Physical exercise has also been shown to release tension and counteract physical fatigue. This strongly suggests that most of the fatigue we experience is not due to physical exertion but rather to our mental attitude (Chapter 11).

- There is a type of chronic tiredness, a form of mental nervous fatigue, which is abnormal. This tension-creating nervous fatigue prevents us from enjoying life. It causes us to be unhappy, which in turn causes us to be more tired. Nervous tension and fatigue are detrimental to our physical, mental, emotional, and even spiritual health.

Tension-creating nervous fatigue can be relieved by adhering to the holistic approach and by practicing affirmation, meditation and positive mental imagery (Chapters 16 and 17). Serious consideration of and making appropriate improvements in your diet and physical exercise programs will foster a sense of well being and counteract any tendency you might have toward tension-fatigue. Worrying also causes nervous fatigue and can destroy your health. Chronic worrying is a symptom of insecurity. It reflects a lack of self confidence. Worrying is a habit and like any other habit can be conquered from within. Learn how to tap your inner source of mental strength and to employ the techniques of positive mental imagery to develop self-confidence and security.

You have the power within yourself to handle stress in a positive manner and to conquer completely the worry-habit, nervous-tension and chronic fatigue.

## Emotional instability: anger, hatred, fear, anxiety, crying spells, etc.

Related to our ability to handle stress is our emotional make-up. Analyze your own emotional make-up so that you may realize how your way of acting or reacting may relate to your ability to cope with potentially stressful situations.

- Emotions can be classified as positive or negative. Where Western cultures view some emotions and situations as being opposites (i.e., love-hate, tolerance-intolerance, peace-chaos, harmony-conflict, etc.), some Eastern philosophies view these as being the same emotion but at different poles. It makes sense to look at some of these in light of Eastern thinking, because then all we need to do when we wish to change an emotion is to shift polarity from negative to positive.

- The negative emotions of fear, anger, hatred, jealousy, sorrow, anxiety, envy and crying spells dissipate mental strength. They can cause tension-fatigue, become self-destructive, and result in your developing not only mental but also physical dis-ease.

  In my opinion, fear is the most powerful negative emotion from which most of the others derive. In analyzing individuals with serious physical dis-eases, fear can be found to be a major causative force. Continued fear does more in perpetuating disease states than any other single negative emotion. Fear causes energy to dissipate, the same energy that is needed to keep body, mind and spirit intact.

- Fear is usually a conditioned reaction to some early unpleasant event. Morbid fears can sometimes be controlled by understanding them.

- Anger and hate are also powerful negative emotions that can make you sick. Only a person who is emotionally immature gives way to outbursts of anger. Expressing anger accomplishes nothing useful. It dissipates energy and causes sickness. If you really think about it, anger does not hurt the person or object you hate. It destroys only the person doing the hating. You can hate your neighbor all you want and it won't hurt him one bit, but what is it doing to you? Anger and hate can eat away at you from the inside. Think about it.

- Selfishness, suspicion, vanity and jealousy are also negative emotions which can make you sick.

- Unhappiness saps vitality. Remember that controlling your negative emotions means conserving your energy.

- Become aware of the reasons behind your fears and hatreds and know that you can love and be tolerant. This will help you to achieve permanent health in mind, soul, and body.

## Mental depression and despair

Mental depression is a self-destructive emotional state which not only results from an inability to cope with stress but also further aggravates your ability to handle life's difficult challenging situations. Some facts about depression may help you be aware of some contributing factors.

- Mental depression is the end result from having frequent unhappy moods and from losing hope. If allowed to progress, mental depression can lead to utter despair. At this point your energy has been exceedingly drained and your ability to recover severely destroyed.

- Be aware of the many causes of unhappiness and depression: being too sensitive to criticism; feeling hurt whenever you feel rejected; becoming irritable when tired; disliking your physical appearance, being too fat, too skinny, and feeling unattractive; being shy around people, lacking self-confidence and worrying about everything; feeling sorry for yourself and seeking sympathy from family and friends; being too suspicious about people's motives; getting quickly discouraged; being immature about accepting ordinary responsibilities; having undue resentment to others and being disillusioned by people; living in the past and being pessimistic about the future; being obsessed with the thought of being a failure and a victim of hard luck; being a health-neurotic and indulging in excessive health-complaining; being obsessed about health-conditions such as ulcers, arthritis, menopause or impotence: etc.

- Depression can result in an ever increasing circle of aggravation. Any physical, mental, negative emotional, and spiritual challenge is capable of influencing the mind. The mind, in turn, can add fuel to the fire leading to further depression.

- Being obsessed with the idea that you are depressed further adds to your depression. If you label yourself as being depressed, you merely reinforce the negative situation or suggestion and your subconscious mind will begin to believe it.

- It is only reasonable to assume that the happier our moods become the lesser the chance of our becoming depressed.

- We must develop a truly positive attitude about our own self-worth. We can bolster our self-esteem. We can achieve this through affirmation, meditation and visualization. However, first believe we can do it.

## Insomnia

In our modern society with its hectic pace, many individuals experience difficulty sleeping. In fact, people who have difficulty sleeping far outnumber those who achieve restful sleep.

Insomnia is a condition which not only results from an inability to cope with stress but also may further aggravate an internal or external state. In addition, it can itself be the stressful situation.

Many individuals resort to sleeping pills and tranquilizers to rest and sleep, not realizing that these drugs actually prevent them from achieving what they really desire. These drugs can be downright destructive and dangerous (Chapter 9).

Some facts about insomnia may help you become aware of some contributing factors.

- Bad sleeping conditions, such as too much noise or an uncomfortable bed;

- Pain and discomfort from an illness such as arthritis, a headache, etc.;

- Nervousness and tension from the day's activities, especially if there was too much excitement or an unpleasant emotional reaction; taking these and other worrisome troubles and problems to bed with you;

- Bad living and eating habits; disorganization in one's living habits causes one's mind to be disorganized.

- Worrying about something that may have happened, or, even more ridiculous, something that is about to happen.

- Feeling guilty about something. Guilt causes you to worry and causes fear which, in turn, causes anxiety leading to insomnia.

- Sexual dissatisfaction can lead to tension, unhappiness, frustration and restlessness.

- As with depression, being obsessed with the false idea that you can't sleep, labeling yourself an insomniac merely reinforces a negative situation or suggestion and your mind will begin to believe it.

Try to develop positive attitudes and habits about conditions in your life and prevent insomnia. A person should eat at a regular time each day, not overstimulate his brain with alcohol, drugs, stimulating drinks, and go to bed at a regular time each night.

Stop worrying about things that are about to happen. Ninety percent of the things people worry about never happen!

Resolve challenges in your private life such as getting to the root of sexual dissatisfaction. Leave your work challenges at work. Talk out problems with other family members and resolve them by bedtime.

Take time to be still and silent. Learn how to meditate and relax your problems away. You will experience restful, restorative, happy sleep. Prepare yourself for a fantastic tomorrow.

## Physical dis-ease

Many physicians and non-medical individuals are beginning to appreciate the fact that many physical dis-ease states have their basis in our negative creative imaginings. The field of psychosomatic medicine developed because there was a need to study the relationship between body and mind. Until recently, there have been only a few physicians who appreciated the fact that physical diseases may have mental causes. Fortunately, however, this number has been growing rapidly. Physicians are now joining the AHMA because at long last there is a professional organization that is devoted to the principle that we do have a body, mind, and spirit, and that the health of the physical body is related to how each of these three aspects of our being work in harmony with each other.

**Cancer.** There is little doubt that the development of cancer is related to your mental and emotional states. The average cancer patient has had some significant physical, mental, or emotional trauma occurring in his life 6 to 18 months (average one year) prior to the development of his malignancy. Many cancer patients are even aware of this event.

The incidence of cancer increases sharply within 18 months after an individual is forced to retire from his job, regardless of his age. Forced retirement is interpreted as a rejection. An individual may feel unwanted and unappreciated. As he begins to feel inadequate, he questions his self-worth, and his self-esteem diminishes. Eventually, the individual develops the feeling of helplessness and hopelessness. Finally, depression ensues. This leads to despair. The subconscious mind loses the will to live. The biocomputer is programmed to self destruct, and the cancer is the way to accomplish the final demise. A grim picture indeed.

The incidence of breast cancer in women increases sharply within 18 months after the last child has left the home — the so-called "empty nest" syndrome. It is then that the feelings of rejection and being unappreciated lead to the final stages of depression and despair.

This whole panorama of negative emotions and feelings is insidious because the average cancer patient is totally unaware of the feelings generated within his or her subconscious mind. It has been shown by Dr. Carl O. Simonton and his co-workers at the Cancer Counselling and Research Center, Fort Worth, Texas, that a person's success in curing himself of cancer is not related to what he thinks he believes, but to his subconscious views. More about this in Chapter 7. It is important for us to develop a way to be in touch with our inner self so that we will know what we really believe. Only then can we make an intelligent decision about what changes need to be made for future growth, development and evolvement.

**Ulcers.** Those who do not appreciate the fact that ulcers is a psychosomatic dis-ease do not fully understand the causes of ulcers. As with other dis-ease states, there are many contributing causative factors, such as mental attitude, undisciplined emotional states, diet, etc. Our mistake in the past has been that we were looking for simple causes. However, we are complex beings and our dis-eases reflect this complexity.

If we were to consider for a moment that we are composed of body, mind, and spirit and that these three aspects of our being are intertwined and interrelated, we can begin to appreciate certain events in our lives. What we eat affects our body directly. It can also affect our body indirectly by influencing how we think and our emotions. Negative emotional states triggered by our overindulgence of caffeine containing beverages, such as coffee, tea, and cola drinks, can result in a increased acid secretion in the stomach and duodenum at times when there is no food within these organs to digest. This constant insult eventually results in the stomach enzymes digesting a hole in the inner stomach lining. Other unhealthy foods and eating conditions can similarly affect our bodies either directly or indirectly by their effects upon our mental attitude and belief systems (Chapter 10).

The stomach and duodenum are final "shock" organs which reflect an imbalance occurring elsewhere in our being. The real problem may be an inability to cope with the job situation, conditions at home with the wife and children, a distorted social life, etc. To focus on the dis-eased organ while ignoring the causes will never result in a successful cure. To mutilate the body by surgical removal of the stomach without a sincere investigation of the role of diet, emotions, mental attitude, and spiritual beliefs reflects a tragic narrow-minded focus on the true meaning of dis-ease. I do believe that we in the medical profession have a responsibility to educate the public about the real causes of dis-ease. We have too long been experts on dis-eases; **we must now become experts on the wellness state.**

**Heart Disease.** The number one killer of man, heart and related cardiovascular dis-eases, is also related to our way of living. We eat too much of the wrong foods. We give only lip service to the need for exercise. We are unable to cope with the every day challenges of our job, personal, and social life. We do not control our negative emotions of fear, anger, hate, etc. Eventually, all of these factors contribute to that first heart attack or the cerebral stroke.

I recently met a gentleman on a train who was recovering from an arterial transplant operation in his leg. He had diverticulitis to boot! His physicians informed him that many of his problems were diet-related, and they instructed him to eat a bland diet. They gave him no further instructions. This man's wife sought the help of a nutritionist who owned a health food store. After talking with the wife, I concluded that the advice of this nutritionist was excellent and I encouraged her to follow it. Although the wife was eager to help her husband (she even enjoyed eating the new foods), he was not so motivated. When they went to a restaurant with friends, he would always order the worst food for himself. On one occasion, the group ordered broiled fish, but not this man. He ordered lobster Newburg with its rich, creamy sauce made with butter, egg yolks, and wine. Later that evening he asked his wife, "why should I have to suffer all the time?"

The fact of the matter is that this man has been suffering, is suffering now, and will continue to suffer because of his dietary indiscretions and hostile and resentful attitudes. He would rather concentrate on what he shouldn't eat than on what he should eat. He feels sorry for himself and he is asking everyone around him to send him psychic energy to help perpetuate his dis-eases (Chapter 7). Some would say he is just where he wants to be. We can observe and learn from this example.

**Other dis-ease states.** There are many other dis-ease states caused by disharmony in the care of our body, in our way of thinking, and in our spiritual lives. In addition to the dis-eases already mentioned above, I believe that all dis-ease states could be viewed holistically with regard to causation and treatment. In my opinion, abnormal conditions such as diabetes, arthritis, multiple sclerosis, headaches, ulcerative colitis, obesity, pain, insomnia, etc. can be controlled and even cured by applying the techniques of affirmation, meditation, and guided imagery to mobilize the intrinsic healing powers.

The purpose of this book is not to discuss how to handle each specific dis-ease, but rather to illustrate by using example how physical, mental, emotional and spiritual dis-ease states are interrelated. Later in the book we focus on the positive side of the coin, that is, how our state of wellness relates to how well we **harmonize** the three aspects of our triune nature.

## Spiritual bankruptcy

Edgar Cayce, the well known psychic healer, believed that the Spirit is life, the Mind the builder and the Physical the effect. What we observe as physical dis-ease or wellness is a state that the mind, consciously or subconsciously (more usually the latter), creates from the abstract level from either a sick or a well spirit.

The spiritual bankruptcy that is being experienced by many in our society is the result of a focus outside of themselves which is directed to material possessions and sensual pleasures. A man who centers his whole life around his family and job may wake up one morning (usually around his fortieth year!) looking for the meaning of life. As he looks at his past he realizes that he has wasted his life building sand castles. He sees himself in middle age having lost a great treasure, his youth. He seriously begins to question where he is and where he is going. He knows where he has been and the prospects of continuing along that path are unfulfilling or downright depressing. He may decide to end his life then, and many do.

Why? Because he has lost hope. He has been living one way so long that he doesn't know a better way. The spirit is like any organ or faculty of the body. If a muscle is not continuously used, it weakens (atrophies). On the other hand, the more it is employed, the bigger, better and more efficient it becomes. So too with the spirit. The spirit has a yearning for growth, development, and evolvement to a higher level of consciousness. If it is not given this opportunity, it stops growing. It may eventually die from what we refer to in medicine as "disuse atrophy."

If we do not exercise our spirit life, we will not be able to cope with potentially stressful challenges. The ability to handle stress directly relates to the resiliency of our spirit. If we go through life bombarded by one and another stressful events and are unable to handle any of them, further insult is added upon injury. The depressed spirit begins to despair.

To continue with our example, the man in his forties may begin to seriously question his way of life. He may think about correcting his course in life. He re-establishes his goals, sets his priorities, and corrects his course. He may have a genuine spiritual awakening. This book is for those who wish to reevaluate their lives for upward spiritual evolvement.

The spiritual aspect is that intangible sense. This is the "feeling" that one receives when any of the physical senses are engaged! To attune ourselves to the spirit enables us to understand ourselves and our surroundings better.

Spiritual bankruptcy is both the end result and the cause of disorganization in an individual's life. Man must develop an active program of spiritual maintainence. The spirit is truly life. It is an integral part of the body-mind-spirit unit. The holistic approach to living fosters self-awareness and teaches self-help. All you need to do is make the decision to do it.

# CHAPTER 6

# STRESS AS AN
# USEFUL ENCOUNTER

## General Aspects

Until now we have dealt with the destructive nature of stress. Realize that what makes stress destructive and harmful is our attitude. Within this universe there are similar forces which may appear different depending upon how we view them, either with a telescope or with a microscope.

The existence of our solar system depends upon a fine balancing of the opposing centripetal and centrifugal forces. Centripetal forces are constrictive. They keep the earth, moon and other bodies in the galaxy together as separate and distinct compact masses in space. The external manifestation of the centripetal force is gravity. Not only does this force keep us here on earth, it also keeps the moon in orbit around us. The gravitational force of the sun keeps the earth in orbit around it. This force is directly proportional to the size of the body exerting the force.

Opposing this is the centrifugal force which is expansive and growing in nature. This force is responsible for the speed of travel of any planet or body in the universe. It keeps the earth and moon traveling in space.

A natural balancing of these two forces keeps the solar system, universe, and galaxy functioning according to the Master's plan. If, for instance, the centrifugal expansive force of the earth traveling were not balanced by an equivalent degree of the opposing centripetal gravitational force of the sun, the earth would continue in space. Life as we know it would cease to exist. If the centripetal gravitational force overpowered the centrifugal, the earth would be drawn into the sun's oven.

Everything on earth is influenced by these forces, especially plant and animal life. In Chapter 10, I describe how these forces influence plant and animal life and how the human being is affected by the forces transmitted by nature into food.

Energy represents a cycling of polarity. If we did not have a positive and a negative, we would not have electricity. Properly balanced and controlled, electricity becomes a useful force in our lives.

The energy within our body and mind must be balanced and controlled. Dr. Robert Leichtman in his essay on *"Coping With Stress"* states:

> *It is helpful to understand that there is an important relationship between conflict and harmony, between chaos and peace, and between imperfection and perfection. These are polar opposites. Conflict results from a lack of harmony; harmony is acquired by conquering conflict and establishing balance in life. Chaos is the absence of peace; peace is achieved by imposing order on chaotic conditions. Imperfection is unfinished perfection; perfection is attained by striving to complete our evolutionary journey. Harmony, peace, and perfection are all more desirable than their opposite poles, but to be sensible, we must realize that they cannot be instantly achieved. We will experience much conflict before we totally master harmony; we will suffer much chaos before we learn the secret of peace; and we will endure much imperfection before we are able to create perfection.*

In my opinion we do not have to experience conflict, suffer chaos, nor endure imperfection, if we don't want to. We can achieve whatever we wish to achieve, when we want to achieve it. If we wish to achieve it now, we can modify our imagination and beliefs. We may begin by re-evaluating our attitude toward the beliefs we wish to replace. To change one's mind is to change the result, e.g., as one turns the tuning switch on T.V. or radio, the program changes according to the chosen channel.

We can look upon stress as a force within our own individual universe. Each of us is the center of our own universe, and within each individual there are physical, mental, emotional, and spiritual forces which are yearning for fulfillment. If these forces are balanced harmoniously then growth and development become a happy and rewarding experience. If, on the other hand, these forces are tugging away from each other, one pulling one way, another in a different direction, then we begin to literally come apart at the seams. We experience disharmony and chaos in our lives.

In addition, surrounding each individual's universe are outside forces that must be dealt with. All forces represent energy. A characteristic of energy is that it is dynamic: it is constantly vibrating, flowing and moving. Each of these forces, as with the energy they are the manifestations of, has a positive and negative end: love and hate; peace and chaos; perfection and imperfection; happiness and sorrow; harmony and conflict. What gives these forces reality is how each of us balances them on the **abstract** level.

## What you reap depends upon what you sow

There is a universal law concerning energy which states that "*energy is conserved.*" It is there all the time. It cannot be created out of nothing! When we think we have created energy, all we have done is convert one form of energy into another. There is stored energy in gasoline which we use to fuel the motor which in turn moves the generator to make electricity. We have converted the energy stored within the gasoline molecule into electricity. Our society depends upon this transformation of matter into energy. The crux of Einstein's theory of Relativity is that the relationship between matter and energy is reversible. Energy can be converted into matter. And, we do this everyday of our lives, albeit in crude ways referred to as work! We use electricity, heat, and other forms of energy to make automobiles, houses, furniture, etc.

Have you ever thought about what happens to the hate energy you send out to your fellow man? What happens to the chaotic energy you emanate? Where does the negative energy you create go? Since energy is conserved, what you create and send forth must be either absorbed by another to be dealt with within his universe, or it can be reflected back to the source, that is, you, the sender. You will then begin to experience the negative situation that you created.

A corollary to the law of energy conservation is the moral dictum that *what we reap depends upon what we sow.* We must really be concerned about the energy field with which we surround ourself. Our positive emotions are sources of positive energy. Just think about how active and energetic we are when we are happy, glad, at peace with ourself and the world, and when we are in love. Our negative emotions cause us to lose and dissipate energy. Remember how we feel when we are sad, unhappy, at war with ourself and the world, and when we are hateful?

Man has been given control over his emotions. We have the free will to be constructive and positive or to be destructive and negative. We have the free will to take another man's hatred, accept it as ours, add energy to it and pass it to others. Then, we begin to reap our own harvest. Eventually, we experience mental and emotional conflicts, spiritual turmoil, and eventually physical dis-ease.

We have the free will to take in another person's emotion, and when we recycle it in our minds, repeat or tell others of it, we give it more energy, thus setting up ourselves for the return or harvest of whatever it was: happy thoughts produce happiness, critical thoughts more criticism, negative thoughts negativity, forgiving thoughts return forgiveness. "**As** you sow, so shall you reap."

When we feel that a person is projecting hatred toward us or others, first let us take a moment to just observe — watch and listen without participating. A fire will die without fuel. Initially, this may be very difficult to do. However, a few attempts at tuning in with openness to what the person is **really** saying behind the words and emotion should lead to more understanding of the situation, thus preventing an all out misunderstanding!

We **are** free to alter another man's hatred, shift the emphasis to the opposite pole of love, accept that love as ours, add energy to this love, and project love to our fellow man. We will then begin to reap that harvest. We will experience mental and emotional tranquility, spiritual peace, and physical wellness.

We reap at the emotional and physical levels what we sow at the mental and spiritual levels.

## Use stress to discover yourself

Much is learned from self-discovery. Holistic health is based upon the principle that we assume the responsibility for our disease or well-being, whichever we experience. Before we can carry out any program of self-help or self-health, let us first develop an increasing awareness about the factors which influence our thinking and learn whether we are an actor or a reactor in life's situations. We must truly discover for ourself what we are, who we are, where we came from, and, finally, where we are going.

Develop a curiosity about your inner workings. Since *stress is a condition, created within you by yourself, of tension and upheaval brought about by your reaction to an internal or external situation,* attempt to discover those factors within you which cause you to view a particular situation as being stressful. You might be so absorbed in learning about yourself that you forget about the stress which caused you to begin the whole process of self-analysis.

So my advice is that when you are faced with a stressful event, ask yourself one very important question: "What is it about myself that makes me react the way I do?" Be sincere about laying the responsibility of **your** actions on **your** own doorstep. **This is the first most important step toward complete integration of body, mind, and spirit and that state of wellness.**

Consider the alternative. The situation may be that you are challenged (or stressed) by something that happened involving a person at work or at home. You complain that this particular person did something to you, or that a set of circumstances is causing you to be unhappy, unloving, and depressed. Open your eyes! Become aware of what is happening to you. You are blaming someone or something outside of you for **your** negative state. Remember when you do this, you subconsciously infer that someone or something outside of you has power over you and your recovery becomes dependent upon that person. This is a very dangerous situation to be in. Maybe, that particular situation causing you to be depressed is not going to change. Then, what are you going to do?

Do not allow yourself to create such a dilemma. What seems to be causing your depression changes when your attitude toward it takes a different perspective.

If you want to remain well, experience joy in your life, love and be loved, begin to take responsibility for your life. Discover yourself. Find out why you react the way you do when you're faced with challenging circumstances. Say to yourself: **I AM RESPONSIBLE FOR MY WAY OF THINKING. I AM RESPONSIBLE FOR MY WAY OF ACTING. WHAT IS IT ABOUT MYSELF THAT CAUSES ME TO REACT THIS WAY. I WILL FIND OUT. I WILL MAKE WHATEVER CHANGES ARE NECESSARY SO THAT I BECOME A POSITIVE THINKING INDIVIDUAL.** Then go on to become the captain of your ship and master of your soul.

# CHAPTER 7

# CONSTRUCTIVE USE OF YOUR MIND IN COPING WITH STRESS

## How the mind functions

Our brain functions as a highly sophisticated bio-computer. Whatever information we take in with our senses (sight, hearing, touch, smell and taste) is indelibly imprinted in our memory bank. The only way this information is lost is when brain cells are lost. Some may suggest that forgetting represents a loss of information. But this is not so. There are reasons why we do not remember.

There are occasions when we've not recalled an incident until someone reminds us of it. The information is stored in our memory bank all the time, only we were unable **temporarily** to retrieve it. Had we utilized our brain more efficiently, had we put that bit of information into our brain cells correctly, had we been thinking with more of our brain, we would have been able to recall the information more easily.

Experts have been using hypnosis to relax individuals who have been able to recall information they could not remember. Hypnosis is being successfully employed to aid witnesses who want to remember details of events involving criminal investigations. The information is not lost. Employing useful methods and techniques can result in information being released from our brain cells when we want it.

Dr. Bruno First, who was a memory expert, said there are two things necessary for a good memory: a relaxed mind and a series of words with which to associate things.

When your mind is relaxed, information flows readily from your brain cells. Meditation, hypnosis, and similar techniques relax your body and mind allowing you to recall information more easily. You may remember times when you have taken a very simple test, such

43

as a driver's license test. You may have been a bit nervous and uptight. There might have been a question, the answer to which you knew, but the more you tried to remember it, the more the answer seemed to elude you. When you left the room and gave a sigh of relief, "Boy, am I glad that's over," then the answer came to you. What happened? Because you were nervous and uptight the information was not readily released from your brain cells, you experienced test trauma. Eventually, when you relaxed, information began to flow readily and the answer surfaced to your conscious mind.

Our minds also function by association. Any method we use to put information into our brain cells, while at the same time relating and associating this information with something else, will improve our ability to recall this information later. Bruno First devised his now famous "Memory Pegs" to help individuals develop their powers of memory by association.

In the beginning of this chapter, I mentioned the brain as a sophisticated bio-computer and now I am discussing the mind. Is there a difference?

## The brain and the mind: Are they the same?

Many people regard the mind and the brain as one and the same thing. Although they are dependent upon each other they are totally different.

The brain is an organ within our cranial vault. It is a physical entity having size, shape, mass and color. The brain emits frequencies which reflect the electrochemical activity going on within it. These brain wave frequencies are recordable on an EEG machine, an electroencephalograph machine. Everyone has four basic areas of these brain wave frequencies as shown in figure 7-1. I will mention them here without going into detail, so as not to digress from the main theme. The four basic areas are: BETA, recordable from 14 and up cycles per second (cps); ALPHA, 8-13 cps; THETA, 4-7 cps; and DELTA, .3-3 cps. These will be discussed later.

The mind part of man, on the other hand, is an abstract entity which reflects through the physical brain. The mind is measurable on an I.Q. test. Appreciate the fact that you do have a mind existing within this body-mind-spirit unit and that this mind of yours is most powerful. Because of the power it has, you must be aware of what is contained within it and what you are continuously putting in it as thought forms.

## The conscious and subconscious minds

Most people don't realize that we have two minds — conscious and subconscious. The conscious mind works only during the times when we are awake and consciously aware. The brain is emitting BETA wave frequencies. The conscious mind can override some subconscious events, such as habit control, but under ordinary circumstances it cannot influence others, such as heart rate, blood pressure, digestion, etc. The conscious mind can be trained to do more than it does. However, rather than letting it take on every little chore, it would be far better and more conserving of energy to have the conscious mind train the subconscious mind.

The subconscious mind, on the other hand, works all the time, 24 hours a day. This part of the mind controls our breathing. It regulates our heart rate and blood pressure. It keeps our intestinal tract working to digest and assimilate food. It does these things without us having to use our conscious mind, and this is good.

If we use our conscious mind to keep our heart beating, what would happen if we remembered to take a breath? Our heart would stop! What would happen if we were to eat lunch and we had to use our conscious mind to control the digestive and assimilation processes? Our heart and breathing would stop! This may sound facetious, but it would probably be true. Whereas the conscious mind can usually direct only one operation at a time, the subconscious can perform many.

In addition, the subconscious mind is constantly working with the information stored within the deeper recesses of our brain. From this complex interweaving of previously stored thought forms, past experiences, and relationships, the mind creates our personality — a personality unique to each one of us.

When all of a sudden we are confronted with a new event, we respond automatically and very naturally in a way determined by our subconscious mind. It, therefore, becomes important what thought forms we put into our mind because the subconscious part of the mind is going to draw from these stored thought forms to develop our own unique way of acting or reacting.

Some people are careful to create positive pictures and thoughts of love and tolerance so that the subconscious mind has good wholesome ingredients with which to mold their personality.

Others are not so careful. They create negative pictures and thoughts of anger, hatred, fear, jealousy, sorrow, anxiety, and envy. These individuals wonder why their mental strength is dissipated, why they experience tension and fatigue, why they develop self-destructive emotions, and why they ultimately develop dis-ease.

We must all be aware of how powerful our minds really are. In addition, we must be aware of what we are putting into our minds for we really *"reap what we sow."* Let us sow constructively that we may reap constructively.

To return to a point made earlier about using the conscious mind to train the subconscious, it would be impractical to use the conscious mind to perform every little function. The conscious mind uses much energy, for it directs the whole body and the conscious mental energy to perform a particular event. Since using the subconscious mind conserves energy, why not train this automatic part of our mind to function the way we want it to? Rather than using our conscious mind to actively suppress what might be an automatic angry response of the subconscious, why not train the subconscious to automatically respond with tolerance? Instead of trying to actively suppress a fear, let us train our subconscious mind to develop confidence in our ability to overcome the challenge. Too many individuals are unaware that the subconscious mind can be a great asset if used correctly. It's like having a great army of minds to rally to our needs. However, it must be developed and trained.

## Background facts about mind power

The mind is a source of energy and it is this MIND POWER which we can use to control all aspects of not only our physical bodies, but also our mental and emotional responses.

As mentioned earlier, the brain emits frequencies which reflect the electro-chemical activity going on within it. Scientists have been able to detect 4 basic areas of brain wave frequencies as determined by electroencephalographic (EEG) recordings. (Figure 7-1).

One area is called BETA. This is a fast frequency range with low energy potential recordable from 14-32 and up cps. This is the brain wave frequency we use to see, hear, touch, feel, taste, and smell. Essentially when the normal individual is awake and functioning at the outer conscious level, BETA wave frequencies are emitted.

The second area, termed ALPHA and recordable from 8-13 cps is one of the three frequency ranges emitted during sleep and while dreaming. This level is also called R.E.M. time area because while dreaming we have rapid eye movement. ALPHA range frequencies, which are slower and more energetic than BETA, are also emitted during meditation and self-hypnosis.

The third area, called THETA and recordable from 4-7 cps, is even slower and more energetic than BETA and ALPHA. THETA brain wave frequencies are detected during sleep and also during deeper states of meditation and self-hypnosis.

The fourth area, DELTA, recordable from 0.3-3 cps, is the state an individual is in while in deepest sleep, coma and deep anesthesia. It is possible to reach DELTA during hypnosis but not very likely through self-hypnosis. Some believe that it may be possible to reach DELTA by meditation, but this requires extraordinary discipline and practice. An important feature about the DELTA state is that, while individuals may appear to be unconscious, in deepest

## BRAINWAVE FREQUENCIES

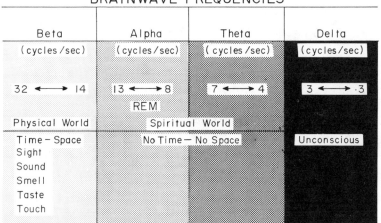

Figure 7-1

sleep, coma or deep anesthesia, they may be able to hear and record onto their brain cells what they heard while in this state. Although they will not have any awareness of what they heard, it still is recorded and will influence their subconscious thinking afterwards.

During meditation and self-hypnosis the brain emits ALPHA or THETA brain wave frequencies, depending upon how deep the individual is within these states. The ALPHA and THETA brain wave frequencies are slower, more stable, and more energetic than the BETA level frequencies. We now know that we can reach the ALPHA and THETA levels while being conscious and that we can employ these stronger, more energetic brain wave frequencies with **conscious awareness** to control bodily functions and to change habits. Equally exciting is the realization that we can go within to the ALPHA level to achieve inner peace-of-mind and tranquility. This is what the use of mind power is all about.

### The three keys to mind power

Mind power is effective when three criteria are fulfilled: the proper and constructive use of our imagination; the development and use of our powers of visualization; and the degree to which we believe it, i.e., our belief factor.

Our imaginations create the thoughts that are processed through our bio-computer. These mental images not only influence our every day behavior, but also become integral parts of us. Since we become what we imagine ourselves to be, it becomes important for us to be creative and positive in our imagination. A positive creative imagery will cause us to be positive, creative and more constructive. Conversely, a negative imagery will result in our being negative and destructive.

Since our mind believes most what it sees, our ability to visualize further influences where our mind power is being channelled. It is reasonable to conclude that we must develop our powers of visualization to add impetus to our positive creative imaginings.

Furthermore, believing in what we create and visualize convinces the mind. Our subconscious inner belief system (i.e. our belief factor) is the important one, and this may be different from what we think we believe consciously. Through meditation we can be taught to know our inner beliefs, and, therefore, we will begin to know ourselves.

Dr. O. Carl Simonton observes that many individuals who are attempting to cure themselves of cancer do not know what they really believe about their cancer. Most of the individuals coming to his center have the attitude that they are going to overcome their cancer, and that they have the will to live. Some are able to control and even cure their cancer; others do not significantly alter the course of their disease and die. Dr. Simonton was interested in knowing the difference between these two groups of individuals. He tells the story of a man who believed he had the will to live and intended to cure himself of his cancer. When asked how he viewed his disease in his imagination, the man described his cancer as a stone wall and his white cells as beautiful white snow flakes falling on the stone wall. This man died. What was this man's imagery really saying? It was saying that deep in his subconscious mind he believed his cancer to be strong — a stone wall — and his white cells were weak — snow flakes. In our county of Frederick, Maryland, we have stone walls that have been in existence for 200 years. The snow has come and gone every winter and the stone walls remain.

Another gentleman viewed his cancer as a big black rat which occasionally would swallow a yellow pill floating in his blood stream. The man was taking chemotherapy in the form of yellow pills. The rat would then keel over and almost die, but soon he would gain strength, breathe more deeply, and get ten times blacker, larger and more ferocious. This man also died. His imagery was saying that he believed his cancer was strong — a big black rat. He also believed his chemotherapy was strong, for it almost killed the black rat. But finally, he believed that the cancer was stronger. The black rat eventually won over the chemotherapy.

Dr. Simonton describes what positive imagery can do. There was a gentleman who entered the center with far advanced cancer.

Chemotherapy was of no avail. In fact, it had almost killed him. Every day this man would send out his team of white knights to kill a certain quota of cancer cells. About four weeks after he started his imagery, the white knights appeared saying that there were no more cancer cells. He told them that he didn't care and that they were to stay out all night searching. Eventually they returned with several more cancer cells. Two weeks later, that is six weeks after he started his imagery, the man underwent extensive testing. The medical doctors could not find any trace of cancer in the man. It is now about seven years later and the man is still free of a disease which in the minds of many is synonymous with death.

I believe that you can be taught to get to know your inner beliefs, and thereby begin to know where you really are.

I further believe that you can be taught to use your imagination in a positive, constructive manner. In addition, you can learn to develop and use your powers of visualization. You can be shown how your belief system affects the use of your mind power. Once shown, you will have the will to modify your belief system to your advantage.

## The power of words

Everytime we say a word we make a mental picture, and it is that picture that is filed into your bio-computer. Electro-chemical activity is produced, the subconscious mind begins to synthesize, and finally new thoughts and pictures are created (many hidden from our conscious reality). Chemicals are sent out to all the cells of the body and the physical body begins to respond accordingly.

We live by every word we utter, according to those chemicals and pictures produced by and within our subconscious. Whether we meant it or not, even if it might have been in jest, we will still live with the effects of what we store within this bio-computer.

Since we are Godlike and created those mental pictures and images, we have power over them. We can cancel out the ones we do not want and recreate a new set of mental pictures to file into the biocomputer, therefore bringing about the conditions we want.

You must, of course, first recognize that you are using negative words and making negative statements. Some of you are going to be amazed at how negative you really are. Many of you have not recognized your own negativity.

The first step toward this mental rehabilitation is to recognize the negativity you are creating and start cleansing it out by feeding in what you do want to create in your life.

You are going to begin to use your imagination constructively. It does take your imagination, just your imagination. Please don't look for the logic behind what we tell you about negative and positive words. You will not appreciate the logic until you have proven it to yourself. Do not allow your logical mind to interfere with your growth and development at this dimension.

Inventors and other creative people frequently make great discoveries because they do not allow logic to interfere with their thinking. We have all heard creative individuals criticized as "crazy" or "illogical," only to recognize one day that they have made a great discovery. That is because they have dared to be different and have not allowed logic to imprison them.

If 200 years ago we were to look up to the sky and see an airplane, we would have concluded that it was either a mirage, a miracle, or the workings of the devil, that it was not possible for something so large and so heavy to fly. It was not logical. We now know that, if we were to follow a set of plans and construct a plane according to specific details set down in the blue prints, it would be illogical if it did **not** fly. Most people apply logic to a specific set of circumstances according to the knowledge available at the time. It is for this reason that it would be far better to keep your mind open to all possibilities so that you can experience life to the fullest.

Logic only exists in the BETA realm. There is no time, no space, no limitation, and no logic in the mind dimension of ALPHA and THETA. Whatever you imagine and visualize or create in the mind dimension of ALPHA and THETA, so it will be in your BETA world reality.

Since there may appear to be no logic to my advice about the use of words, I am going to tell you a story to show just how you may use your imagination constructively. There was a man who died and left an inheritance of 11 cows to his three sons. It was stipulated in his will that the oldest son was to get one half of the inheritance, the next son was to get one quarter and the youngest son was to get one sixth. However, they could not butcher a cow. The father felt that they should be wise enough to figure out how to divide the 11 cows and keep to the letter of the will. The brothers became bitter enemies over this for they were unable to solve their dilemma. Finally, after about a year, they found a wise old man in town, and they went to him and explained their challenge. The old sage looked it over and said, "Sons, I can readily see that you have no challenges at all. All you have to do is to use your imagination." He said, "Go to your imaginary world and borrow a cow now making your total 12 cows. So the oldest boy will get one half, that is six, the next will get one quarter, that is three, and the youngest boy will get one sixth, that is two. When you add these up you get 11. So you just send the imaginary cow back to where you borrowed it from to begin with."

Solving situations in life can be as simple as learning to use our imagination constructively. We are creative beings. This fact separates us from lower animals. Because we have the power to create, we need not feel that we must compete with our fellow man. Let us put our energies toward becoming creative thinkers.

When you catch yourself using words and phrases that may be limiting you, begin to use your imagination. Say to yourself: cancel, cancel; erase, erase. Imagine that you have an eraser in one hand with which to erase a word or phrase from the blackboard of your mind. Now rephrase what you want in a positive manner, so you can have what you want without limitation.

You should begin by cleaning up your language, especially those dirty four letter words! Table 7-1 lists a series of negative words, words that conjure up negative images, and alternative positive words and phrases which can be used instead. Think for a moment of the powerful negative programming which occurs when you use the word "can't". Most people will forget about attempting to do the feat at this point. Imagine the programming which occurs when you use the words "nervous" and "anxious". Realize how much better you can feel when you use the words "eager" and "creative energy" in their place. Contemplate each one of these negative words and the suggested positive alternative words or phrases.

### Table 7-1
### Negative Words and Alternative Positive
### Words and Phrases

| Negative Words | Positive Words and Phrases |
|---|---|
| The dirty 4 letter words | |
| 1. can't | 1. can |
| 2. lost | 2. misplaced (temporarily) |
| 3. damn | 3. blessed |
| 4. poor | 4. dear |
| | |
| 5. if | 5. I will |
| 6. doubt | 6. expect the best |
| 7. maybe | 7. positively |
| 8. anxious | 8. eager |
| 9. nervous | 9. creative energy |
| 10. forgot | 10. slipped mind (temporarily) |
| 11. problem | 11. challenge or situation |
| 12. worry | 12. concerned |
| 13. cheap | 13. reasonable |
| 14. broke | 14. out of cash flow |
| 15. sorry | 15. apologize |
| 16. stress | 16. challenge |

Table 7-2 lists some of the commonly used negative phrases and alternative helpful suggestions. Don't use them any more. Replace them every time they surface. Rather than concentrating on the negative with such a phrase as "Don't forget," state it in a positive manner by saying, "Please remember." Do not conjure up the negative emotions of fear, being scared, experiencing pain, etc. Your subconscious mind will soon get the pictures and these negative emotions will surface at a time when you are challenged and can least afford the drainage of energy.

### Table 7-2
### Commonly Used Negative Phrases and Alternative
### Helpful Suggestions

| Negative Phrases | Helpful Suggestions |
|---|---|
| 1. Don't foget | 1. Please remember |
| 2. I am scared or I am afraid | 2. Calm and fearless |
| 3. I am afraid I couldn't do that | 3. I bet I can do that |
| 4. Scared to death | 4. I am fearless |
| 5. So afraid I could die | 5. Give me strength |
| 6. So happy I could die | 6. So happy I could celebrate |
| 7. Tickled to death | 7. Tickled to laughter |
| 8. Sick and tired | 8. Well and relaxed |
| 9. My heart is broken or | 9. Heart is happy |
| 10. My heart is all torn up | 10. Heart is cheerful |
| 11. A pain in the neck or | 11. A comfort in the . . . |
| 12. A pain in the you know where! | 12. A comfort in the body |
| 13. I can't see why | 13. I **can see** why it works the other way |
| 14. I don't have the time | 14. I will make the time |

Note: To replace these command phrases consciously is to re-groove a new record until they become automatic at the unconscious level producing the **desired** result automatically. Since the subsconscious mind is said to be a **willing servant** of the conscious mind, it carries out orders literally.

Begin to protect yourself from your potentially worst enemy, yourself. Many times you have to convince yourself before you can convince others. From now on when someone asks how you are, your reply will be: "I am better, better and better."

Begin to call and refer to your children by positive names. Do you really want them to become such things as: dummy, stupid, fool, turkey, etc.? If you don't, then don't call them by those names. In my pediatrics office a very common name fathers call their sons is "turkey." What a name! I cringe every time I hear it. A turkey may be one of the dumbest birds in the world! These parents are unaware of the power of words.

Refer to your children as genius, brilliant, beautiful, and love because these are what you really want them to be.

Think about positive names to call your husband or wife. Envision in your own mind just what you want them to be: sweetheart, lover, etc.

Be aware that our Creator made everything perfect. The imperfections that we have in the world are figments of our imagination which we have mis-interpreted and to which we have given energy. If we have imperfect bodies, we have probably somehow created it most likely at the subconscious level. If we have imperfections in any area of our life, it is also likely that it surfaced from a level of unawareness. So let us now take responsibility for our thoughts and actions. Self-realization is the first step toward self-awareness. Realizing that you are the cause of your being opens the door of increasing awareness about yourself.

From now on when someone asks how you are, what is your answer going to be? Better, better and better. Emile Coué said, "Everyday in every way I am getting better, better and better." At first you may feel a little bit awkward saying it because it is strange and unfamiliar. But, I assure you that you will begin to reap the benefits of your creative positive thinking. The mental images you are getting is that every day in every way all things **are** better, better, and better. And, isn't this what you want?

## How to reject negativity and create positive situations

As you begin to go out in the world with your positive attitude saying better, better, and better, you are going to get some very interesting comments. Firstly, you may realize that your well meaning friends really didn't want to know how you really are. They asked you because it was a habit or just a courtesy. When you came back with something positive, it jars them momentarily. Remember that what you are saying is unfamiliar and strange to them, and that most individuals either shy away from the unfamiliar or get hostile. They reject this new approach as being either evil and sinful or the mark of someone who is "losing his marbles." These individuals recognize and feel comfortable only with the familiar. They are used to having others say: "Oh! Let me tell you . . ." and go on into an organ recital — usually organ by organ! And they are used to hearing about their no good spouse, children, boss, etc.

Another facet of this situation is that you shouldn't let others put their limitations on you: "Don't you feel well? You look terrible. Did you have a bad night?" Your subconscious mind begins to get the picture, and in a hour or so, you go home sick because you allowed others to put their limitations on you. You can learn to reject the negativity of others and send it back to them with love!

There are times when I have to say to people in my presence, "I reject your negativity." There are times we must physically do this so the subconscious mind gets the picture that we are rejecting it.

The mind is very powerful. It runs our whole existence. When we agree with something, we have accepted it, we have computerized it, and we will eventually live it.

When you listen to the aches and pains of others and you agree either outwardly or silently by listening, you add psychic energy to these negative thoughts. Similarly, when you talk of your aches and pains to others, they add energy to your dis-ease conditions.

Remember to alter any negativity which you may be perceiving by emphasizing love and project this love to both yourself and your fellow man. There may be times when you have to remove yourself from negative situations by having your legs and feet move the rest of your body physically away from the source of negativity.

Some may ask at this point what if you are a health professional and it is your job to listen to the aches and pains of others? Or is there any value in listening to a friend in trouble with the purpose of soothing him or her? In both situations do listen, but with a certain emotional detachment that allows you to send positive vibrations to your client, if you're a health professional, or to your friend. You can listen and be a source of positive comfort.

In my opinion, there is potential danger to empathizing and sympathizing. When you empathize you share feelings and emotions and you may become de-energized in the process. You are consumed by negative energy. There are many physicians, especially psychiatrists, who eventually get sick, and many commit suicide, because they fail to realize that we have an energy field around us, and not only can we affect others by our thoughts, but we also are affected by the thoughts of others around us. When you sympathize you send pity to others and you add more psychic energy to their mental, psychological, and even physical dis-eases.

As a health professional and as a friend, learn to listen with a certain detachment. Conserve your energy. If you have spiritual beliefs, picture yourself as an instrument of God's infinite strength flowing through you to your client or friend. Picture them well and whole, not as sick and disrupted.

The image you have will go out to your client or friend and you will have done them considerable good. This you would not have done if you wallowed in their negativity. Eventually, you will learn how to be an instrument of good, a channel of energy, and your clients and friends will derive strength from you.

Have you ever been in someone's presence and become drained of energy? You may have wondered why you begin to feel tired. This is because negativity is draining and saps your energy and strength. It lowers your resistance so that you become increasingly susceptible to infections and other dis-ease states. You literally become sick and tired. You lose your ability to handle challenges and you become further depressed.

Most individuals can remember someone they have known who gave off "negative vibes," and while in their presence you become affected by their energies. You want to leave and go away from them. Nobody wants to be around a negative person. Negative people keep bringing up the past. If you didn't like the past the first time you experienced it, why keep talking about it now. When you do, you are recomputerizing the very conditions you do not want in your life. Guess what you will soon experience? Yes, the very thing you wish to avoid. People enjoy talking negatively about their ex-husbands or ex-wives. And, did you know that many eventually re-marry individuals similar to the persons they divorced? The reason is because they constantly talk about and recomputerize the very negative conditions they do not want. The negative situations become more familiar and most individuals find security in the familiar. Eventually, they attract to their conscious reality an individual similar to the person they divorced.

There is hope! All is not lost! From now on when you walk into the presence of someone who wants to wallow in their negativity, and that is all they want to talk about, you are going to say, "Oh, Oh, Oh, O, O, O, O." Stand back and block out their negativity. Eventually, they will sense your reluctance to add energy to their negativity, and they will lose their enthusiasm in telling you their negative story. Try it. It really works.

When you agree with someone's negativity you curse that person. Everyone who listens has drawn a mental picture for them, which is there for yourselves also.

It is really true that when you cry, you cry alone. On the other hand, when you laugh, the whole world laughs with you. Everyone wants and enjoys being around a positive person.

You all know individuals whom you enjoy being around. They are positive, uplifting, happy, lovable and full of joy. You experience the same positive emotions while in their presence. You can be a source of joy and happiness to yourself and to others. All you have to do is put your mind energy to it.

So, begin talking about the positive conditions you want in your mate, your children, your bosses, your fellow workers, your subordinates, and everyone. Watch everything change. *What you experience is directly related to how* **you** *perceive it.* If you talk about the shortcomings of your mate, remember that everybody within hearing distance is adding energy to it and helping to compound the situation. And, wait till you get home! What you may encounter is the monster you, with your friends' help, created. So let those within hearing distance add energy to the positive conditions you wish to experience. Your life will be enriched accordingly.

## Biofeedback

A chapter about how the mind functions would not be complete without a discussion of biofeedback. In 1958, Joe Kamiya, a noted psychologist was looking at EEG patterns in a sleep project which he was conducting. He asked his subjects to let him know when they thought they were in ALPHA or not in ALPHA. By the third hour, most of his subjects were able to indicate correctly whether they were or were not in the ALPHA — and biofeedback was born. Essentially, the biofeedback machine is a device which indicates to you, the subject, when you have achieved the ALPHA state.

Considerable research has been done with biofeedback, especially by Elmer Green and his associates at the Menniger Foundation, Topeka, Kansas. It has been and continues to be a superb research tool in teaching us how the brain and mind functions. Many individuals are being helped by the reinforcement they derive from the biofeedback machine.

Although we employ biofeedback in our research, we would rather have an individual concentrate upon developing a belief within himself, so that he or she can achieve the meditative state without dependence upon a device.

The biofeedback and EEG machines detect brain waves coming from the outer *cortex*, the so-called *grey matter* of the brain and the seat of our conscious mental functions. The subconscious mind is centered in deeper levels, probably in the so-called *limbic* area, beyond the reach of these instruments. Although there appears to be a correlation between what goes on in the outer *cortex* and the inner *limbic* areas, it is not 100 percent. This is the reason why the hypnotic state cannot be defined by EEG readings.

Quieting the conscious mind of extraneous perceptions and focusing conscious mental energy, both of which happen when you achieve the ALPHA state, allow you to make contact, enter, and influence the deeper levels of your subconscious mind. The **most** important factor in achieving what you desire is developing and maintaining a positive belief within your subconscious mind. Dependency upon a device may, in some circumstances, prevent you from achieving this goal.

## Conclusion

To deal with stressful situations, learn *constructive use of your mind.* You must first recognize that you create your whole life: your perception, your attitudes, your emotions, your likes and dislikes, your loves and hatreds, your fears, and so on. Once you believe this, and you should because it's true, you are ready to accept the responsibility for **your** life. You can then begin to increase your awareness of the individuals and things around you, and of your God. You must then devise a plan of developing positive attitudes. This can only come from within, because you perceive the world and yourself using your imagination. Start **now** to develop a positive imagination. Then learn how to use your mind's eye, your power of visualization, to impress what you desire upon your subconscious mind. Develop and maintain a positive belief system, perhaps the most important key to mind power. Do not deviate from your course. Keep your eye on your goal and power your drive at your full potential of creative energy.

You are then ready to experience life as it is intended: beautiful, joyful, and full of Love.

# CHAPTER 8

# HOW TO USE STRESS AS A POSITIVE FORCE

**Physical, mental, emotional and spiritual growth
related to stress and challenge; How to use your
challenges for growth and understanding**

Is there anything within a situation that makes it a challenge?
Usually not. What may be a challenge for one person may be a
blessing for another. I hope to convince you that all challenges are
blessings, some in disguise.

Reverend Bob Stevens, a Unity minister in San Diego, California,
always bellows: "Oh, thank you, God, for problems!" Is he crazy? Is
he some Unity minister who has gone off the deep end? I'm happy
to say, he is not. He is, in fact, much aware of how the mind and
spirit function and how you must use your mind constructively.

If challenges exist and there is nothing within the challenge making it so, then, what makes a situation a challenge? It is you, the
individual facing the particular situation or event who labels it a
challenge for yourself. By so doing, you create that challenge with
your imagination, thus giving it reality. It is your perception of the
situation which makes it real to you.

Don't misunderstand me. I am not saying that challenges do not
exist. They indeed do exist. You create them, but that in itself is not
bad. It is how we deal with a particular challenge which will determine whether it will be a destructive force or a positive force
causing you to grow into a higher level of consciousness.

Oh, yes. Thank God for challenges, for they indicate to us an
inner inadequacy that needs correcting. Let us go within to our
inner being. Find out why we are reacting the way we do to create
the challenges in our life, then determine what it is we must do to
overcome the challenge and grow accordingly.

59

Our greatest growth usually occurs during and after times of great stress and storms. Challenges, storms, stress — whatever we wish to call them — should inspire us to seek another way. They should make us come to grips with what is lacking within ourselves.

Stop blaming other people for your inadequacies. Stop saying "Why did he or she do that to me? The world has done it to me again. Poor little me." This attitude is self-destructive and shifts the blame away from you, when in reality the responsibilty is yours.

Let us stand up straight and assume the responsibility for what we are doing and what is happening to us. We do create both the good and the bad in our lives. Often individuals take the credit for their achievements. "Look what I did today. See what I can accomplish when I put my mind to it! I've done this and I did that." You hear this sort of bragging all the time. This is human nature. There is nothing wrong with standing up and taking the credit for the good things that happen to you. There is nothing wrong with liking yourself, realizing your own assets, and having confidence in your powers.

But what kind of songs do individuals sing when they fail? "I was shafted by my fellow worker or a friend. I was robbed of this or that opportunity. I was passed over for a promotion because the boss liked someone else, etc. Poor little me. I'm such a good man. I don't steal. I'm honest. Look how this cheat won over me. It isn't fair."

These are funeral songs. They are cop-out attitudes. Go within and find out why you've failed. Maybe you have an inner inadequacy which must be worked upon. Maybe you're in a dead end job and another promotion may entrench you more in that dead end job. Maybe you have other talents the Universe wishes you to develop. Maybe **God** wants to get your attention. Singing these funeral songs leads you away from the real source of your challenges. It focuses the blame away from you, when in reality you should go within and find out why you are doing this to yourself or why this is happening to you. There is a reason for everything that happens to you. You may not at the time appreciate the Force guiding you toward an unrecognized goal. Have faith, be positive, and be determined that you will find the reasons behind a particular disappointment.

I'm reminded of the time I left the National Institute of Health where I was a research scientist to go into private practice. There were circumstances beyond my control, as I thought at the time, which caused me to leave the job I loved. I had the job I wanted to die in. What a negative imagery! In fact, I did die in the job but didn't realize it at the time. I died morally and spiritually. I decided I had to get away from it so I went into private practice — something

I thought I would never do. After all, I was programmed in medical school to consider teaching and research the ultimate goals for an enlightened physician. Private practice was mundane and for graduates of lesser medical schools! With these thoughts filed away deep in my subconscious bio-computer, I went into private practice. I never did what I wanted to do in research. My dream from the time I was in prep school would probably never become a reality. There was a conversation going on within my head between me and someone else who appeared to live there also. I'm sure you have all had similar conversations! This other voice — if I am allowed the liberty of calling it a voice without completely losing my credibility — told me that I would one day return to the work which would lead me to the fulfillment of my dream. I thought this was absurd because going into private practice was in the opposite direction to what I believed had to be the course toward fulfilling the dream. It was not until four years later, after having been plagued by cluster migraine headaches, and having successfully cured myself using meditation, that I realized that I was going in the correct direction. I am now well on my way to fulfilling that dream, and writing this book represents part of the work I've been doing to make that dream a reality.

What appeared to have been the greatest disappointment in my life turned out to be one of the greatest blessings. If I had remained at that job at NIH, I would now be doing the same type of research I had been doing and probably not anywhere near what I really wanted to do. I had actually deviated far from my goal and from the purpose of why I had gone into medicine in the first place.

Use your challenges to learn about yourself. Analyze your disappointments, problems, and the negative situations in your life. Try to find out the **real** meaning behind the things that happen to you. Accept the challenge with a positive living spirit. Ask, "Okay, where do I go from here?" Trust that the Universe has a grand design, and that you are a part of the all-knowing, all-loving, all-powerful Master's plan. Often, you must get beyond yourself to allow the Creator with His infinite wisdom to work you into His grand design. Keep your options open. Don't be afraid to leave the old and open the door to the unknown. You would have never begun to walk had you not ventured beyond your crib. You may have fallen many times in the process of learning how to walk, but you learned quickly. Now, you can run, skip, and jump.

Close the door of your past, for your past is what's limiting you. Don't keep recomputerizing the past unless you want to relive and re-experience it. Putting your energies into past events will prevent you from going forward.

Open the door into the future. Jump into a new exciting world.

The universe is infinite. It has no limits. There are infinite opportunities out there waiting for a creative being to develop. Leap into this new world. You may discover that you can fly.

## Attitude can mean victory or defeat

Many individuals experience success and victory because they envision and expect only success and victory. They do not harbor doubts in their own minds. Doubts short circuit and drain your mental energy so that you **cannot** achieve your goal.

On the other hand, many individuals are constantly experiencing failure and defeat because of their negative attitudes. You may know some of these people. They constantly complain, "I can't do this" or "I can't do that," and you know they aren't doing anything, except, of course, to fail. This is because they are expecting failure. Faith and belief work both ways: it gives you your successes and your failures.

When I applied for entrance into the Harvard Medical School, I was a senior at Boston College. I received two post cards notifying me that I had to appear at two separate interviews. I attended the first, and I was satisfied with the interview.

The second interview was scheduled one month later. I wondered why the two interviews were so far apart. On the day before the second interview I noticed that the day of the week and the date printed on the post card did not coincide. The two did coincide for the previous month. I called the medical school to notify them of the error. I was informed that since I had not attended the second interview my application was removed from consideration. They were good about it, however. They realized **their** error and re-scheduled me for a second interview on the Friday after Thanksgiving with Dr. F.

I told my advisor at Boston College about the events leading up to this second interview. When he found out I had an interview with Dr. F. he gave me his condolences and told me that no one from Boston College who had been interviewed by Dr. F. had ever been admitted into Harvard Medical School. He was a tough interviewer, and apparently was prejudiced against Boston College students. I decided I would appear at the interview and give Dr. F. a *run for his money!* At that point I felt that I would probably not get admitted, but, at least, I would have *my day in court.*

It was raining on the day of the interview. I came about 30 minutes early and waited in the lobby of what was then the Boston Psychopathic Hospital. I wondered whether this was an omen of what was to come! But, I was committed (not to the hospital!) to what I had to do that day and I felt confident I would survive the interview.

While I was waiting in the foyer, a tall man entered the hospital, checked in at the reception desk and disappeared down the hall. He seemed to know where he was going. It was Dr. F., although I didn't know it at the time. Five minutes before my interview was scheduled, I went to the reception desk and announced my presence. The receptionist called Dr. F. on the phone. There seemed to be some angry words and an unhappy mood. The receptionist turned around and told me Dr. F. would come to get me shortly. Within minutes he arrived, not very happy.

He asked me: "Weren't you here when I came through the lobby?" I answered: "Yes." "Well," he said, "Why didn't you let me know you were here? You made me come all the way down stairs to get you and it was unnecessary." I told him although he had a picture of me (submitted with my application), I did not have one of him, and I would have been more than capable of finding his office by myself if I were so directed. He mumbled and grumbled some more. I paid little attention to him.

We took the elevator to the second or third floor of the new wing of the hospital which was not yet completed. He directed me around the corner, down the hall and into his office which contained a desk, two chairs, and a blackboard. As soon as we walked into the room he pivoted around and asked me: "Why don't you hang your raincoat up? Most civilized people do hang them up, you know." I told him that if there were a coat rack I would. He took me by the arm, out of his office, down the hall in the **opposite** direction from which we came, and around a corner to another elevator. There beside the elevator door was a coat rack. I nonchalantly flipped my coat on the rack. I was beginning to wonder whether it was time to wake up from this dream (or rather nightmare). When we returned to his office the real fun began.

He directed me to sit down in the chair. He handed me a familiar form to sign. I had to sign a similar one at my first interview. Essentially it stated that I swore that I was who I claimed to be. He handed me the form. He threw a ball-point pen across the desk toward me, and told me to fill it out with my pencil. The pen rolled off the desk and onto the floor between my chair and the door. I made no attempt to pick it up. I let it remain just where it was as I proceeded to complete the form **with my pencil.**

Dr. F. looked over my records and told me that I had done poorly in the mathematics portion of my medical aptitude exam. If he had said English composition or history, I might have believed him. But, mathematics, no. I was a whiz at mathematics, and I told him so. He told me I was wrong, and that he wanted to check it out.

He proceeded to draw three U-shaped containers on the blackboard. He told me that one beaker contained four cc's and another three cc's, and he wanted to know what combination of each of these I would use to get 11 cc's in the third beaker. I asked him if the beakers were calibrated. He looked me straight in the eye and asked me if I were some kind of wise guy. I told him that calibrated beakers were readily available and it would be easier to use them rather than play these "silly games". He told me he didn't care what I thought and to do the problem as he instructed. So, I told him to use two of the four cc beakers and one of the three cc beakers to get 11 cc's in the third beaker. He asked me to do two additional problems that were equally simple. Afterwards, he told me that he felt there was nothing wrong with my mathematical abilities and he couldn't understand the test results.

We made some small talk about sports, the holidays, etc. He dismissed me. I thanked him for the experience and walked out the door, making it a point to act out my stepping over his ball point pen as I left the room. I never looked back.

On the following Tuesday at 10:00 p.m. I received a telegram from the medical school admissions committee, congratulating me on my acceptance into the Harvard Medical School.

I did not realize until three years later what the interview was about. It was the first day of my third year in Psychiatry rotation. Guess who the instructor was? Yes, it was the one and only Dr. F. He asked me how I was, and told me he was always confident that I would make it through medical school.

He accompanied us, myself and four other students, to his office. It was the same office in which I was interviewed. However, an adjoining conference room which had been empty before now had a conference table, chairs and built-in bookcases. In his main office there was a coat rack!

As I sat in the conference room waiting for the class to begin, I reached over to the lowest shelf of the bookcase behind me and picked up a reprint of an article Dr. F. had published. My eyes almost popped out of my head as I read the title: "Effects of Stress Interview Situations upon Incoming Students to the Harvard Graduate Schools." There had been many "guinea pigs" in this experiment. The stressful interview situations were contrived!

What were Dr. F's conclusions? Those students entering the Business College were the most relaxed and withstood the pressures of the interviews the best. Next were the prospective law students. The least relaxed were those being interviewed for the Medical School. He concluded that prospective medical students were immature, uptight, and fell apart easily when stressed by the interviewer.

What lesson did I learn? I wasn't going to let anyone push me around. I never did anyway. If I had gone into the interview with a defeatest attitude and allowed him to reduce my psyche to ashes, I would not have been accepted. My act was one of confidence and strength. The lesson here is to create an attitude which will reflect what you hope to achieve. If you wish to win, your attitude must reflect victory. If you wish to cope with and use stress as a positive force for growth, development, and evolvement, then develop a positive attitude of strength and confidence in yourself and visualize your goals as already accomplished.

# CHAPTER 9

# THE DESTRUCTIVE TRANQUILIZERS

## General aspects

Man has within himself a built in system of checks and balances which operates to keep the body and mind functioning properly. This is called *homeostasis* which is defined as the tendency to maintain normal, internal stability in the organism by coordinated responses of the organ systems that automatically compensate for environmental and internal changes. This system is so finely tuned that interference usually results in harm to the body.

There are systems which increase our heart rate and blood pressure to accommodate the increased needs of our muscles when we are physically exerting ourselves and exercising. There are systems that cause increase blood flow to the skin to help us lose heat in the summer time and to decrease that blood flow to conserve heat when it is cold outside. When we eat, the body shifts blood away from the muscles and to the intestinal *portal* circulation to help in the digestion and assimilation of our foods. In the bright sunlight the pupils of our eyes constrict and in the dark they dilate so as to allow the correct amount of light for us to see. There are many more homeostatic control mechanisms working all the time, to which you give no thought at all. We stated earlier that our subconscious mind works 24 hours per day controlling all these things for our well being.

We are beginning to realize that the use of tranquilizers interferes with our body's internal mechanism to deal with stress. In case you might think that you've read incorrectly, I'll repeat this. *Tranquilizers which are supposed to help you deal with stress actually work against our built in system designed to help us deal with stress.* This chapter is intended to convince you that this is so.

## Damage caused by tranquilizers

**Tranquilizers, sedatives, and narcotic drugs can mask impor-
tant symptoms of serious dis-ease.** This reminds me of a personal
event occuring in my life when I was attending medical school.
Shortly after Thanksgiving of my first year, I developed a bout of
severe abdominal pain associated with diarrhea. After several
weeks I went to student health and with no examination the physician informed me that I was experiencing spastic colitis due to the
nervousness of being in medical school, the competition, etc. This
was compounded by the fact that I was eating highly spiced Italian
foods. I acknowledged that I was always a high strung individual
and that for most of my life my blood pressure had bordered in the
150 systolic range, but why all of a sudden did my "shock organ"
change? (my blood pressure now, 23 years later, is 104 systolic / 60
diastolic and my resting heart rate is about 55.) I had always had a
strong intestinal constitution having been able to tolerate all of the
bad, hot and spicy foods we Italians eat! He told me that body conditions change with age and he was satisfied his diagnosis was correct. From the last week of November, 1956 to June, 1957 I do not
believe that I had more than 3 or 4 normal bowel movements, the
usual being severe diarrhea associated with moderate intestinal
pain. In June, the physician prescribed deodorized Tincture of
Opium which I proceeded to take for the next two years. About one
year later I started to experience low grade fevers in the afternoons.
Because student health was not open in the afternoon, I went to the
clinic in the morning to inform my physician of the low grade fevers. He took my temperature which was normal. I told him it was
always normal in the morning. He patted me on the back and told
me that everything would be OK, to go back to classes and try to
relax. He had already branded me a crock! I was determined not to
return to the clinic. However, something happened in the spring of
1959. The pains increased in severity, my temperature rose to
higher levels and I got to the point where I could not function very
well. But, my deodorized Tincture of Opium kept me happy! One
morning with a temperature of 106 degrees Fahrenheit, I strolled
into the clinic. My physician couldn't ignore that temperature! He
didn't. My faith in medicine was restored! To make a long story
short, I was admitted into the hospital and eventually underwent an
exploratory laporotomy. What I had was a pelvic appendix, not one
that was in the traditional right lower abdominal area. When I got a
mild bout of appendicitis, the colon, which was adjacent to the appendix would get irritated resulting in the colitis symptoms. When I
rested, the inflammation in the appendix would subside and I would
feel better. Ultimately, I had ruptured the pelvic appendix, and my
new symptoms of very high fevers were the result of the abscess,

which was difficult to explain on the basis of "nerves"! There were numerous complications after surgery. I will not go into the details, other than to comment that such things happen to medical students. My advice to medical students is, "Don't get ill while in medical school. It may not be in your best interest!"

I'm also reminded of Larry who was 16 years old when I first met him. He had been on Valium for one year to control attacks of hyperventilation. His mother had attended a workshop I presented on "The role of body, mind, and spirit in holistic healing." She was concerned about her son being on Valium. She asked me whether I could cure her son using meditation. I told her Larry could cure himself of hyperventilation if he learned how to meditate and applied himself toward this goal. Larry came and attended a mental training program our Center sponsors called T-H-E-M-E (Total-Holistic-Enrichment through Meditative-Enlightenment). We attempted during the week of the course to wean Larry from his Valium.

Larry had been to his family physician who made the diagnosis of hyperventilation after being told by his nurse who had seen one of his attacks that it was hyperventilation. Larry was given a paper bag to breath into, a commonly accepted method of treatment. He was then sent to a neurologist who preformed an EEG and some other tests and concluded that there wasn't anything he could do to help. Larry was then sent to a pediatric psychiatrist who prescribed Valium which appeared to lessen the severity of the attacks.

On the last day of the T-H-E-M-E seminar Larry was doing fine although he informed me that he had had one of his attacks. That evening he had a longer one. When his mother described the event, I began to have questions about the diagnosis being correct. I was not his physician and had no reason to question the diagnosis which I knew had been confirmed by both a neurologist and a psychiatrist. Two days later Larry was still experiencing his hyperventilation attacks. I suggested that his mother allow Larry to come to my home where I could teach her son more specific imagery and possibly might have the opportunity to observe one of these attacks. Larry came one evening and during supper had a most peculiar attack — something I had never seen before. I wasn't sure what it was, but I knew what it was not. It was not hyperventilation. Within 30 minutes after his first attack in my home, Larry had what appeared to be a grand mal, a generalized, convulsion. Again, it was the most peculiar convulsion I had ever seen. Larry was asked to use mental imagery to control these attacks which he had almost every 20 minutes while he was awake. He was able to control every one of them after that by employing imagery. This, however, was not getting to the cause.

The following morning I admitted Larry to the hospital, performed more tests, and concluded that Larry had a brain tumor, the symptoms of which had been successfully suppressed by Valium while his tumor grew larger and larger. He underwent a successful operation, the tumor was removed, and now Larry is doing well.

There is one very important difference between using your internal mechanisms to control symptoms of dis-ease and employing medicines and drugs. The former works with other internal stabilizing forces. Drugs may work against such homeostatic tendencies. Let me explain.

Larry was able with meditation to control his convulsions. If he were able to check and possibly destroy the tumor by mobilizing his internal immune mechanism, his symptoms would have disappeared completely. This was not attempted because of the advanced nature of the tumor and its location in a vital area of the brain. He would not have been able to completely control the seizure symptoms by meditation while the tumor continued to grow. The body's innate wisdom overrides any other internal regulating mechanism that may interfere with vital elements. Meditation and positive mental imagery are safe.

The use of drugs, on the other hand, is not. Tranquilizers, such as Valium, narcotic pain killers, and other drugs can override key body warning mechanisms. This was the case with Larry. The Valium did control the seizures, but the brain tumor continued to grow. It was fortunate that Larry's mother was not satisfied that Larry had to take Valium indefinitely.

**Tranquilizers, sedatives, and narcotic drugs have many adverse side-reactions which can be more devastating than the dis-ease being treated.** To illustrate this I will relate the story of the mother of a member of the Board of Trustees of our Center. This lady was 75 years old and she had a mild stroke. In order to decrease the ability of the blood to clot and possibly prevent another stroke, her physician prescribed aspirin, a common well-accepted mode of treatment. She started to experience severe gastric discomfort, most likely due to the large doses of aspirin she was consuming. Her physician then prescribed Librax to treat the gastric symptoms.

Within a few days the mother of this dear friend of mine had a complete psychotic break. Her physician interpreted this as representing a progression of her basic disease which had caused the stroke.

Her son wasn't satisfied. He suggested that her psychotic symptoms might be related to the Librax. His mother's physician said it couldn't be so, but that he would check with a local psychiatrist to be sure. Within minutes he called back stating that these

types of reactions had been noted from Librax. He had been unaware of this before.

You have no idea of the chill that went up and down my spine as I
listened to this dear old lady who had been lucid up until the time
she took the Librax (and I considered myself a well-seasoned
physician). The Librax was discontinued, and in about two weeks
her psychotic symptoms cleared.

Let us for a moment look at the advertisements Roche Products
Inc. publishes in the medical journals about their product, Librax.
Firstly, under the section on Indications, it states: *Based on a review of this drug by the National Academy of Sciences – National
Research Council and/or other information, FDA has classified the
indications as follows: "Possibly" effective: as adjunctive therapy in
the treatment of peptic ulcers and . . . . Final classification of the
less-than-effective indications requires further investigation."*

Do you understand what they are saying? They are saying that
Librax is ' *"possibly" effective!* ' They aren't even sure of its effectiveness and they are recommending its use!

Under the section of Adverse Reactions Roche states: *"When
chlordiazepoxide HCl* (the scientific name for Librium, a major
component of Librax) *is used alone, drowsiness, ataxia (staggering
gait), confusion may occur, especially in the elderly and debilitated;
avoidable in most cases by proper dosage adjustment, but also occasionally observed at lower dosage ranges. . ."* There is more.
Carefully scrutinize the ad on page 72:

Note that over 90% of the printed information in the advertisement
is devoted to Contraindications, Warnings, Precautions and Adverse Reactions! The adjoining page of the original ad telling you to
use Librax was done in six colors. Believe me when I say that most
physicians never get beyond the colored page.

Wouldn't you rather learn how to mobilize your own God given
intrinsic powers to overcome your physical mental, emotional, and
spiritual challenges, than resort to drugs which can do harm to
both your body and your mind? Your answer should be yes. If it is
no, read another book.

## Tranquilizers, sedatives and narcotic drugs are addictive

Much of the advertising of these drugs state that with usual dos-
ages the problem of addiction does not occur. This is false. Addiction almost always occurs after long term use of about 3 to 4
weeks. The degree of addiction, however, is usually dose related.

For instance, if you were to take 2 to 5 milligrams of Valium 2 to 4
times per day for 3 weeks, and you were to decide to stop taking
the drug you may experience agitation, probably more so than

when you started. You have actually become dependent upon the drug. You are using the drug as a crutch rather than face up to the real challenges of life. Upon withdrawal you may experience diffi- culty sleeping, find it hard to concentrate, and become irritated at little things that didn't bother you before. Your family may even notice it and suggest you take your Valium.

If you were to take up to 50 to 60 milligrams of Valium per day and you stopped abruptly, you would experience epileptic seizures. This type of withdrawal indicates severe addiction and is the type recognized by physicians. It is dramatic. This type of withdrawal requires hospitalization as in the case of an individual coming off "hard" narcotics.

The central nervous system gets used to these drugs and eventu- ally becomes dependent upon them. It may well be that tranquiliz- ers suppress the natural mechanisms to deal with emotions so that when the drug is stopped, it requires time for the body to regener- ate the enzyme systems needed for the natural system to work.

Why not use your body, mind, and spirit holistically? Learn to activate your own internal system of checks and balances. The more you use them, the better they will function. Dependence on addictive and dangerous chemicals can and does suppress your own natural homeostatic systems.

## The suppression of natural defense and treatment mechanisms

Tranquilizers and other psychotropic drugs are powerful chemi- cals which interfere with brain chemistry. We now know that the body makes substances called *endorphins*. These *endorphins* are chemically indistinguishable from narcotic drugs such as mor- phine. Now, I ask you, "What is the body doing making morphine- like drugs?"

Well, it appears that we have an internal mechanism to control pain. When we need to mobilize it, we can cause our own body to produce these narcotic-like *endorphins* which go to the site of in- jury or dis-ease and relieve pain. They are produced in many areas within the body, both within the central nervous system of the brain and spinal cord and in areas associated with the peripheral nerves. These substances enter the blood stream and arrive at the site of action where they must attach to specific receptors. In fact, this is how they were discovered. Researchers performing investigations on how morphine works within the body discovered specific recep- tors for morphine. They wondered why the body contained recep- tors specific for morphine, a drug extracted from the poppy pod. Did God in all his wisdom create these sites so that when man dis- covered morphine this drug could work? Probably not. So they

suspected that the body produced its own morphine-like substances to accommodate the specific receptors. Amazing deduc-
tion! And it was true.

Once the receptors are full, it may take a day or so to regenerate
the receptors again so that the *endorphins* can attach and work.
This is the reason why after several days of administering morphine
derivatives to a patient with chronic pain the drug doesn't work for
a while. This is also the reason why acupuncture goes through a
refractory period when it doesn't work in a patient with chronic
pain.

Exciting research is now being done to investigate how the release of these naturally occurring pain control substances can be
triggered by deep massage, acupuncture, acupressure, meditation,
biofeedback, etc. Isn't it interesting that you have within your body
a mechanism to produce pain killing substances. You also have the
ability to release these substances when **you** need them by using
the power of **your** mind through concentration and meditation.
What more would you want? Do you really need morphine and
other pain killing drugs?

It is also interesting that you have the built in mechanism to produce other substances, those related to *endorphins,* which affect
your moods and your ability to cope. The release of these substances is also internally controlled.

Taking drugs such as Valium, Darvon, and other psychotropic
and tranquilizing drugs interfere with the body's intrinsic mechanism to relieve pain and deal with emotional challenges. Darvon
has a morphine-like chemical structure. It attaches to the specific
receptors without releasing pain. It does, however, block the *endorphins* from attaching, thus preventing the internal system from
working.

A few months ago a patient came into my office and told me a
story of what happened to her 8 years previously. At the time she
was involved in what she describes as "an impossible marriage."
She eventually developed what her doctors diagnosed as multiple
sclerosis. Soon afterwards, she began to experience mild pain, for
which her physician prescribed Valium.

Almost as soon as she started taking the Valium, her pain intensified to a point where she was really suffering. Her physician interpreted this as being further progression of her basic multiple
sclerosis dis-ease process, and he prescribed the narcotic codeine.
This resulted in her being dopey. Meanwhile, her pain continued.

Finally, she lost faith in her doctors. She stopped taking all her
medicines. She began to feel alert again, her pain disappeared, but
her multiple sclerosis progressed.

She eventually separated from her husband and took her children to make a new life for herself. She remarried, her personal life became happy once again and the symptoms of multiple sclerosis disappeared completely. She has been free of symptoms and any demonstrable dis-ease for almost 7 years.

She told me that she tried to convince her physician that Valium intensified the pain, but he wouldn't listen to her. Why do many physicians concentrate on the disease process? Why don't they consider the potential side reactions of the drugs and other additions to the therapy? Maybe it's because physicians are experts on dis-ease. Should they rather be experts on wellness? This is food for thought which we will discuss later.

## Exciting information from mind and brain research: Right vs. Left Brain

The brain is a most interesting organ. The abstract entity, we call the mind, is even more fascinating. Researchers are now discovering that both sides of our brain do not function in the same way. We apparently have a right brain and a left brain, a right mind and a left mind. Let me explain.

Most of us know that one side of the brain controls the muscles on the opposite side: the right side of the brain(RB) controls the left side of the body, the left side of the brain(LB) controls the right side. Usually, one side of the brain is dominant: most people are right-handed indicating LB dominance; fewer people are left-handed indicating RB dominance. Although there are a few individuals who appear to be ambidextrous (they use either hand equally well) you can usually detect a slight difference, indicating their preference to use one hand.

In an individual who is right-sided and whose LB is dominant, the LB is associated with logical thinking, deductive reasoning, mathematics, information derived from the physical senses, etc. The RB of these individuals is associated with non-spatial events, psychic talents (e.g. ESP, precognition, psychokineses, telepathy), creative dreaming, inventing, poetry writing, etc. With the left-handed individual these conditions are reversed: the RB is concerned with logical thinking; the LB with the psychic non-spatial talents.

Our society and educational system concentrates on developing the LB of an individual, slowly but surely making the RB inactive from disuse. We tell a child to disregard his dreams and be more logical. Children who are talented in the arts, we compel to excell in mathematics. We do little to develop the creative RB talents. Later in life, when we are searching for the true meaning of life, we are unable to use that part of our mind which is concerned with these thoughts. We have suppressed RB activity so much that it becomes a real chore to recover from the years of stagnation.

The brain and mind functions as any other organ or talent we may have. If you do not use a muscle for any length of time it atrophies, that is, it shrinks, each individual muscle fiber gets smaller, and we get weak. On the other hand, muscles grow and get stronger from the stimulation of exercise and use.

The more we use the faculty of memory, the better we are able to memorize. When I was taking second year college English, my professor made us memorize poetry all year long. We started with 10 to 15 line poems, and the last poem we had to memorize was Francis Thompson's *The Hound of Heaven,* all 183 lines of it. Believe it or not, it was easier to memorize the 183 lines of this poem than it was 20 lines of a poem given us in the beginning of the year. Our professor admitted at the end of the course that the poems he gave us to memorize were not important. What he wanted us to do was to develop our faculty of memory. He believed that the more we used such a faculty, the better it would function. He was so correct.

The more we use and develop our psychic talents, the better we are able to use these aspects of our mind for self-analysis, self-development, and any degree of self-help, including self-health. This is essentially what this book is about: developing our inner self for growth, development, and creative living. I believe these are RB functions. In addition, I believe we can further develop these heretofore inactive talents of our RB and mind by using meditation, positive mental imagery, and the belief factor.

Make an effort to develop the other half of your mind. It is the silent half, the half we have not been taught to use, which holds the key to creative living.

# CHAPTER 10

# HOW DIET AFFECTS STRESS

## General aspects

There is no doubt in my mind that the food we eat affects the quality of life. Diet influences our physical, mental, emotional and even our spiritual health. The basis of holistic health is to bring the three aspects of man's nature—that is, body mind, and spirit — into harmony, so that man becomes a whole "I" or "holy". He essentially functions as a whole person, rather than as three separate schizophrenic entities working against each other.

The relationship between diet and health is something to which I formerly gave little attention. After all, in medical school what we were taught about nutrition could probably be put on the end of a pin! The information we were given about nutrition did not go much beyond teaching us that there are carbohydrates, proteins, fats, and vitamins, and considerable detail about a process called "intermediary metabolism."

In April, 1977, the importance of diet was brought home to me in a rather personal way. I had been preparing myself to give a meditation course, and I was reading books on diet. I came across George Ohsawa's book on *Zen Macrobiotics,* and what I was reading sounded great, if it could be believed, yet so bizarre.

It was a small book and I read it several times. The more I read it, the more bizarre it sounded. You must remember where I was coming from: a rather traditional Italian immigrant home with its pastas, tomato sauces, meat, pastries, and espresso coffee, and a traditional conservative Harvard Medical School training. If I were to believe George Ohsawa, I not only had to ignore what I had been taught in medical school, but I also had to almost reject my heritage. At the time, I wondered whether my psyche would survive two such traumatic insults and remain sane!

Can you imagine giving up eggplant, tomatoes, the not too Italian sweet potato, and regular potato? How about giving up meat, sugar, heavy spices, and white flour? Yes, that included giving up Italian bread and pastries. How about giving up coffee? I had been drinking 10-15 cups of coffee by noon each day and I used to drink espresso coffee as a nightcap! Many evenings I would go to bed without the espresso and couldn't go to sleep because I was awake and even agitated. If I got up, made myself a pot of espresso and drank it, I would then be able to sleep "like a baby." What I didn't recognize at the time, but do now, was that my symptoms of agitation, not being able to sleep, increased nervousness, etc. were actually the symptoms of withdrawal — caffeine withdrawal.

George Ohsawa was proposing a macrobiotic diet — macrobiotic meaning the great life. His book is good reading for historical perspective and for the general macrobiotic philosophy, but for content and recommendations, there are better books which are more moderate, and in my opinion, more reasonable, in their approaches to this way of eating.

If you gave up all these familiar foodstuffs, what would you get in return? What Ohsawa promised could not have sounded more like a charlatan's approach to a state of health.

He promised a feeling of well-being; a relaxed and healthy attitude about life in general; a good night's sleep; a more enjoyable satisfying sex life; a peaceful attitude. If you were aggressive (and that I was!), you would lose your aggressive behavior, but your determination would be strengthened. I asked myself, how could this be? I had always believed that aggression and determination went hand in hand. Ohsawa further promised that the ability to think clearly would be enhanced. There were many other things he promised, all equally bizarre to my way of thinking.

I always considered myself an adventurous individual. So, I decided to go on a macrobiotic diet for 30 days, if for no other reason than to prove Ohsawa wrong and to strengthen my traditional medical beliefs and my Italian heritage.

The first 10 days I ate only brown rice, then I started to expand my diet to include other similar culinary delights! I was into the third week of the diet when I realized that I had lost weight. I was more relaxed. I was experiencing a great feeling of well-being. I was sleeping as I usually do. Many of my professors could verify that I had no challenges sleeping through their lectures. And I was experiencing something I had never expected. The depth of my meditation increased and what I could accomplish in meditation was changing (growing). The clarity of my thinking improved. I stopped reacting to outside challenges. My relationships with other people improved. I was becoming less aggressive, and guess what? My determination to achieve the goals I set out for myself increased. I began to realize the true value and capabilities of my inner strength.

I won't describe what was happening to my sex life! I'll leave that up to your imagination!

All this by the third week. I said to myself; if I feel so good, so alive, so vibrant, so fantastic, why would I ever go back to what I had been eating before? The answer was that only a fool would. A fool I have never been, or would ever admit to be. I then developed what can best be described as a modified macrobiotic diet. And, I hardly ever cheat!

I have since studied much about the effects of diet, investigated and evaluated many diets. I still feel that I can objectively and scientifically evaluate the pros and cons of these diets. I also feel that my studying has just begun.

I have concluded that I had been ignorant of the value of diet and its effect on health. In addition, I believe that many professorial level nutritionists are even today more ignorant than I had been back in early April 1977.

## How diet affects physical health

We are becoming increasingly aware of the fact that our basic physical health is related to what we eat. A discussion of the relationship between diet and physical health would require a book to describe. However, we would like, at least, to go into some detail about several dis-ease states to make you appreciate that the health of our physical body is directly related to the food we eat.

In his testimony at the U.S. Senate's Select Committee on Nutrition and Human Needs, Dr. Mark Hegsted, Harvard School of Public Health, stated that there is a great deal of evidence, and it continues to accumulate, which strongly implicates, and in some instances proves, that the major contributing factors to death and disability in the United States are related to the diet we eat. Conditions related to diet include coronary heart disease which accounts for nearly half of the deaths in the United States, several of the most important forms of cancer, hypertension, diabetes, and obesity, as well as other chronic diseases. During the same hearings, Dr. Theodore Cooper, Assistant Secretary of Health, estimated that about 20 percent of all adults in the United States "are overweight to a degree that may interfere with optimal health and longevity." Obesity due to over-consumption of food in general has become a major public health problem not only itself but also as it relates to cardiovascular diseases.

**Heart disease prevention and treatment.** Of the 10 leading causes of death, cardiovascular and related diseases far surpasses all others. The 1969 census lists diseases of the heart as #1 (364.1/ 100,000 deaths), vascular lesions affecting the central nervous system (i.e. strokes) as #3 (102/100,000), and general arteriosclerosis as #8 (16.7/100,000) — giving a grand total of 482.8/100,000 for cardiovascular-related diseases. These rates have increased steadily in the last 10 years.

We now know that heart disease begins at an early age and the ultimate heart attack is the end result of a continuous series of dietary insults. Autopsies performed on soldiers who died in the Korean War revealed that otherwise apparently healthy and fit (by external standards) 20 year old men had considerable arteriosclerotic (i.e. fatty cholesterol-laden) plaque formations in the major vessels coming from the heart. Since then, similar plaque formations have been observed in younger individuals. It takes years for these plaques to develop, and so that by the time you reach your mid-40's and early 50's the plaques have extended into the coronary arteries which bring oxygen and nutrients directly to the heart muscle. This potentially dangerous situation is compounded in many individuals by cigarette smoking. The nicotine contributes to a physiological narrowing of the arteries already partially obliterated by fatty-laden plaques. There is a biological law that states that constant insults to the body will result in deteriorating health conditions (GOTACH Biological Law #2)

Evidence relating heart disease to diet include:

- The level of saturated fat has been directly linked to excessive level of cholesterol in the blood and, therefore, to heart disease. A famous prospective evaluation, better known as the Framingham study, concluded that, of all the risk factors in heart disease, the strongest and most consistent risk factor was elevated serum cholesterol concentration;

- A high cholesterol intake in laboratory animals resulted in arterosclerosis;

- Atherosclerotic disease appeared to decline in Scandinavian countries during the war years when consumption of calories and animal fat declined;

- Southern Italians who emigrated to the United States develop the typical American higher blood levels of triglyceride and cholesterol as they become able to afford the high-saturated fat, high-cholesterol American diet;

- Comparisons among populations with wide ranges of average cholesterol intake show a close relationship between dietary cholesterol and serum cholesterol concentrations.

It is now widely accepted that a high dietary cholesterol intake is a major determinant of the high cholesterol concentrations found in the U.S. population as well as in other technically developed countries.

There is hope, however. The beauty of nature is that when you remove the insulting causes the body will begin to reverse the disease process and heal itself. At the Longevity Institute in Santa Barbara, California, Nathan Pritikin has devised a program of diet and exercise whereby individuals with serious heart disease are started on a fantastic road to recovery and cure. He admits all forms of cardiac invalids, individuals who can't walk five steps without having to take nitroglycerine pills, others who are incapacitated and ready for cardiac bypass surgery. These individuals spend one month at the Institute, learning how to eat a diet containing 10-15% total calories from fat. The modern American diet has a fat content of 40-45%. They walk and jog miles each day. After one month these cardiac invalids can rapidly walk or jog 5 to 10 miles without symptoms. They are essentially returned to normal function. All this from a combination of diet and exercise.

Initially, the American Medical Association, the paragon of health in these United States, was critical of Pritikin who is not a physician. The program was criticized because many nutritionists believe you cannot live on a diet of 10-15% fat. That's funny! The Hunzakuts in the Himalayas and the Vilcabambians in Equador don't know that, and they not only survive but also enjoy excellent health on such a diet. Soon after CBS's "60 Minutes" televised a show on Pritikin and the Longevity Institute, Pritikin got a 2-page spread in the *AMA News,* the official organ of the AMA.

The fact is that you can not only **arrest** but also **reverse** the deposition of cholesterol fatty-acid plaques that is the cause of occluding your coronary arteries. These individuals coming out of the Longevity Institute and other similar programs are curing themselves because they have the consciousness to rise above their old habits of eating the wrong foods, and because they are willing to exercise. They are working to achieve better health, and they are curing themselves.

It is true that there are individuals who eat eggs, butter, and beef and who have high blood-cholesterol levels, yet who live long lives apparently free of cardiovascular disease. Recently, investigators have found that fats are carried through the bloodstream by a series of lipo-protein molecules of which there are two types: low-density lipoproteins (LDL's) and high-density lipoproteins (HDL's). If there is more cholesterol than is needed for daily metabolism, some of the LDL's may deposit their fatty molecules on the interior lining of arteries. The HDL's, on the other hand, have the ability to pick up the excess cholesterol and carry it to the liver for excretion from the body. It has been found that long-lived individuals have very high blood levels of HDL's when compared to other family members who died earlier. Some investigators are convinced that the higher HDL/LDL protective ratio is genetically determined and that one family in 500 may have this natural protection.

The recent conclusion that you can create a more favorable HDL/LDL ratio by diet is exciting. Dr. Edward Kass and a team of Harvard Medical School researchers evaluated the blood pressure of more than 200 individuals eating a macrobiotic vegetarian diet in Boston. Not only were their blood pressure readings well below both the local and national average for their age and sex, but virtually every one of these subjects also had an extremely high HDL/LDL ratio. Dr. William P. Castelli, Director of Laboratories for the Framingham Heart Study, who collaborated to perform the serum lipid (fat) study, concluded that a low-fat, low-cholesterol diet can have almost the same effect as a favorable genetic trait. A prudent diet which emphasizes vegetables, vegetable oils, cereals, fish, little meat, and **no** junk foods, such as fatty hot dogs and potato chips can accomplish the same as a totally vegetarian diet.

Similar conclusions were drawn by the Select Committee on Nutrition and Human Needs. Evidence was presented there showing that diets high in complex carbohydrates may reduce the risk of heart disease. High carbohydrate diets are quite appropriate for both normal individuals and for most of those with hyperlipidemia (high blood fat levels), provided that the carbohydrate is largely derived from grains and fibers. On this diet an energy excess is not consumed and obesity does not result.

Simply stated, if we follow a diet more in line with what nature has intended for the human body to consume, we would be spared the ills of cardiovascular diseases. We should appreciate that the final heart attack is the end result of a long series of dietary insults over a period of 40-50 years. It behooves us to develop the habit of eating health-promoting foods so that we will enjoy a long healthy life.

You don't have to wait until you're a cardiac invalid. Start eating a healthy diet. Combine this with a program of aerobic exercise (Chapter 11). Begin to experience health again.

**Cancer.** There is increasing evidence suggesting that cancer (the #2 killer) is not only diet-related but it can also be prevented and possibly even cured by dietary means.

The proverbs, *an ounce of prevention is worth a pound of cure* and *prevention is the best medicine,* are universally valid in matters of health. In fact, most individuals will readily accept these statements as sound and reasonable. Why then do most people not practice prevention? Of the many possible reasons, two stand out:

lack of motivation and human arrogance that "it won't happen to me." A person who has developed lung cancer from smoking will be motivated to quit smoking, but, by that time, it is too late. We are ever hopeful that, once presented the evidence, the intelligent individual will realize that he does have the power to create both his good and bad health conditions.

There is considerable evidence suggesting the relationship between diet and cancer:

- Obese individuals have a higher than normal risk of developing cancers, particularly of the breast, gall bladder, and endometrium (inner lining of uterus). In laboratory studies the increased risk of cancer has also been demonstrated in overweight mice as compared to control mice of normal weight.

- Mormons and Seventh-Day Adventists who eat little or no meat enjoy much lower rates of cancers of the breast, uterus, colon, and rectum than comparable groups of other Americans who eat meat diets. The vegetable protein diet of Mormons and Adventists are high in fiber and roughage.

- In African countries where the diet is high in grains and other fiber-containing substances, cancer of the intestinal tract is extremely rare.

- In most countries where deaths from cancers of the colon and breast are uncommon, diets are low in animal and dairy fats.

- Cancers of the colon and breast are uncommon in Japan where the traditional diet contains little meat and almost no dairy products.

- The risk of developing cancer is significantly reduced in mice whose protein and calorie intake is restricted.

- Japanese who migrate to Western countries and adopt the native Western diet significantly increase their risk of developing cancer of the breast and colon. Within a few generations their risk equals that of the rest of the population.

There are several explanations as to why diets rich in animal proteins and fat increase the risk of cancer and how an increase in dietary fiber might possibly protect against it.

There are studies which suggest that the normally occurring intestinal bacteria break down the animal fat and cholesterol into toxic substances that can cause cancer. Since the gut is constantly exposed to high concentrations of these toxic substances, it becomes highly susceptible to the cancer causing effects. Some of the toxic substances are soluble and, after being absorbed into the blood stream, are carried to distant organs causing damaging effects there. Cholesterol can be metabolized and converted in the body to form hormone-like compounds which may act like certain hormones that are known to cause cancer in animals. The cholesterol molecule is the basic structure of many body hormones, such as cortisone, the sex hormones (estrogens and testosterone), and many others. An imbalance of some hormones can result in susceptible cells going wild and becoming cancerous; hormone-related compounds absorbed in the gut may interfere with the delicate balance the body strives to maintain.

High fiber diets fill you up more easily causing you to consume fewer calories. This helps to prevent obesity and may reduce the risk of cancer. Also a diet rich in grains and vegetables increase the bulk of the intestinal contents. The transit time within the gut is shortened and the toxic substances are eliminated rapidly and do not remain in contact with the cells of the gut lining as long as would be the case when the gut contents move along sluggishly.

Some authorities (e.g., Doctors Gio B. Gori of the National Cancer Institute and David M. Hegsted of the Harvard School of Public Health) are recommending a significant change in the typical American diet. Early in 1977, the Senate Select Committee on Nutrition and Human Needs recommended similar changes:

- A 25-percent reduction in the consumption of fats and a 25-percent increase in native carbohydrates, such as whole grains, vegetables, and fruits instead of sugar-sweetened foods. A switch to a more vegetarian diet will result in less cholesterol and fats in your blood, less difficulty in controlling your weight, better control of your blood pressure and possibly less risk of getting cancer.

- Avoid deep-fat frying. Instead, bake, boil, broil, roast or stew. If you must make soup or stew using meat stock, cook it ahead of time and chill it. Then you can discard the fat that congeals at the top before reheating.

- If you must eat meat, select lean cuts and trim off all visible fat before cooking. Remember, that a basic vegetarian diet is much more healthy. Eat less high fat, beef, lamb, and pork and more fish and poultry.

- Substitute skim or low fat milk and cheeses for whole milk products. Eliminate butter and substitute soft margarine. Use only liquid vegetable oils such as corn, soybean or safflower. Eliminate eggs from the diet.

The chapter on this subject is not yet closed. More and more evidence is accumulating and it all suggests the same thing: our modern American diet which is rich in animal fats and protein significantly increases the risk of developing cancer and a diet rich in grains and vegetables not only reduces the cancer risk but also the risk of heart and vascular diseases.

**Obesity.** As mentioned earlier, in testimony at the July, 1976 hearings of the U.S. Senate's Select Committee on Nutrition and Human Needs, Dr. Theodore Cooper, Assistant Secretary for Health, estimated that about 20 percent of all adults in the United States "are overweight to a degree that may interfere with optimal health and longevity". In fact, more than 70 percent of the U.S. population can be classified as obese.

What is the cause of obesity? It is the over-consumption of food. This has become a major public health problem. Many professionals in nutrition and medicine agree that today's diet no longer matches the increasingly sedentary life Americans lead. Not only are they eating too much, they are also eating the wrong foods. The proportion of calories from the three basic food energy sources have shifted significantly since the early 1900's; fat consumption accounts for about 43 percent of the total calorie intake, up about 25 percent since 1900; carbohydrates have decreased to 45 percent, down about 10 percent; protein intake has remained about the same at 12 percent of total calories. Significant also is the change in carbohydrates from the more complex types to refined sugar and alcohol.

Current dietary trends may also lead to malnutrition through under-nutrition. Fats and sugars are relatively low in vitamins and minerals. Consequently, diets designed to control weight and/or save money, but which are high in fat and sugar, are likely to lead to vitamin and mineral deficiencies. Low income people are particularly susceptible to inducements to consume high-fat/high-sugar diets. Our claim to be the best fed nation in the world might be valid if a livestock judge were evaluating our physique prior to sending us to slaughter! The American diet of pizzas, hamburgers, macaroni, TV dinners, cheese, peanut butter, cookies, soft drinks, etc. is a far cry from what our bodies should be consuming. This diet contains too much refined sugar and flour, cholesterol and fat, and too little native carbohydrates and fiber.

Ironically, medical science has taken the credit for wiping out such nutritional deficiency dis-eases as scurvy, pellagra, rickets and beriberi, dis-eases which would not have developed were it not for man's interference with nature. When civilized man decided to polish rice and not eat the whole grain as nature had intended, the dis-ease, beriberi, appeared. Medical scientists discovered that this dis-ease was due to thiamine (vitamin B1) deficiency which was corrected by adding thiamine to the diet — the same thiamine that was contained in the whole rice grain and had been discarded by polishing. A similar situation occurred when prison inmates in the

United States were fed refined corn. They soon developed pellagra, due to niacin deficiency — a dis-ease which would not have developed if natural whole grains were consumed.

I contend that nature provides appropriate and wholesome foods for man to eat. Man's interference with the laws of nature brings chaos and dis-ease.

How can we best prevent and control obesity? It is simple but not simplicity. The success of any diet program depends upon developing and establishing permanent eating habits that are conducive to maintaining a healthy physical body. Good eating should replace bad eating habits. If you diet during the week so that you can splurge on the weekends, controlling your weight is doomed to failure.

Of course, it is well accepted by most that obesity is related to over-eating. And obesity is one of the major challenges many individuals wish to solve. The amount of money being spent by obese people to lose weight and control their eating habits far surpasses that being spent to control any other habit. Unfortunately, many obese individuals are looking for the easy "one or two pills a day" or a simple "glass of appetite suppressing drink" to solve their weight challenge. Success is eventually achieved when they realize that it is the totality of what and how they eat that is causing their obesity and when they get serious about correcting the real causes.

If you have a tendency toward being fat and overweight, you must remember that the average fat person cannot achieve permanent weight loss and control by diet alone. You must regularly exercise aerobically in order to lose weight and keep it off (Chapter 11).

The purpose of this section was not to discuss all the dis-ease states affected by diet, but rather, to make you appreciate the principle that diet does affect our physical health. Hopefully, you will begin to become more aware of dietary factors, to increase your knowledge about diet and health, and to make the necessary changes to improve your way of eating.

## Effects of diet on mental, emotional and spiritual health

Diet not only affects our physical health; it affects the quality of our everyday life, how we feel, how we think.

It affects our emotional responses. Do you have a tendency toward depression? Go ahead. Take a shot of alcohol and see how depressed you can really get. Do you have a tendency toward being hyperactive and having jittery nerves? Go ahead. Continue to drink stimulating drinks such as coffee and continue to eat refined sugar and see how much more nervous you'll become.

Are you quick to anger, are you aggressive, and do you devour other people bringing their wrath down upon you? Continue to eat red meat and you will continue in your aggressive behavior.

Diet affects the way we think, and the way we think, in turn, affects the way we cope with stressful situations. As mentioned earlier, we create most of our challenges ourselves. Eating foods and drinking beverages which make us nervous, irritable, grouchy, and unpleasant will affect our behavior with our fellow man, who, in turn, will react to us creating an atmosphere of tension and frayed nerves.

The mistake we have made in the past with the use of tranquilizers is that we thought drugs would help calm our nerves and cause an improvement in our ability to handle stressful situations. Here we have diet on the one hand causing us to swing way over to one side, then drugs to help us swing back over to the other side. We subject our bodies to wide swings here and there hoping somehow to achieve the so-called happy medium road to stability.

It's like taking cyanide and the antidote mixed together. The mixture would not kill you, but would you drink it? Of course, you wouldn't. If you didn't swing way over to one side, you would not have to take a chemical to bring you back to normal or to make you swing way over to the opposite side. Besides, chemical drugs actually prevent you from facing your challenges in a way that allows you to learn and grow from the experience.

Obesity is a challenge with which many individuals are faced. They are overweight, which, causes them to become nervous, which then results in their overeating and more obesity. How can you achieve inner peace, if you don't like the way you look?

**Diet is the most important factor in keeping your physical body healthy.** When your body is ill, your mind soon becomes ill, then your emotions are affected. The reverse is also true. When your mind is ill, your emotions are affected. Eventually, your body develops dis-ease.

## The diet controversy: The U.S. Senate Select Committee on Nutrition and Human Needs' *Dietary Goals for the United States*

There are as many diets as there are experts, as there are cultures, and as there are individuals. Discussing diet is almost as bad as talking about religion and politics! Not even the experts agree.

The U.S. Select Committee on Nutrition and Human Needs made a significant contribution to nutrition in this country when they published the *Dietary Goals For the United States.* In this document were published the seven dietary goals:

1. *To avoid overweight, consume only as much energy (calories) as*

*is expended; if overweight, decrease energy intake and increase energy expenditure.*

2. *Increase the consumption of complex carbohydrates and "naturally occurring" sugars from about 28 percent of energy intake to about 48 percent of energy intake.*

3. *Reduce the consumption of refined and processed sugars by about 45 percent to account for about 10 percent of total energy intake.*

4. *Reduce overall fat consumption from approximately 40 percent to about 30 percent of energy intake.*

5. *Reduce saturated fat consumption to account for about 10 percent of total energy intake; and balance that with poly-unsaturated and mono-unsaturated fats, which should account for about 10 percent of energy intake each.*

6. *Reduce cholesterol consumption to about 300 mg. a day.*

7. *Limit the intake of sodium by reducing the intake of salt to about 5 gram a day.*

These goals suggest the following changes in food selection and preparation:

1. *Increase consumption of fruits and vegetables and whole grains.*

2. *Decrease consumption of refined and other processed sugars and foods high in such sugars.*

3. *Decrease consumption of foods high in total fat, and partially replace saturated fats, whether obtained from animal or vegetable sources, with poly-unsaturated fats.*

4. *Decrease consumption of animal fat, and choose meats, poultry and fish which will reduce saturated fat intake.*

5. *Except for young children, substitute low-fat and non-fat milk for whole milk, and low-fat dairy products for high-fat dairy products.*

6. *Decrease consumption of butterfat, eggs, and other high cholesterol sources. Some consideration should be given to easing the cholesterol goal for pre-menopausal women, young children, and the elderly in order to obtain the nutritional benefits of eggs in the diet.*

7. *Decrease consumption of salt and foods high in salt content.*

The Senate Select Committee could have deserved unqualified congratulations and praise were it not for their subsequent actions. The Committee's report of the *Dietary Goals For the United States* published in February, 1977, with its courageous and sound recommendations was vigorously opposed by segments of the food industry hardest hit by the recommendations. The cattle industry protested the suggestion to cut back on red meat. Egg producers fought the idea of reducing egg consumption. The sugar industry presented their evidence that sugar was safe at current levels of consumption. The dairy industry also rebuked the report.

Ironically, the American Medical Association, siding with the food industry, contended that insufficient evidence existed to support the need for, or the benefit from, major changes in the national diet as proposed. However, the American Dietetic Association gave the recommendations their unqualified endorsement. No wonder the public is confused.

In response to the food industry's opposition, the Senate Select Committee came out with a subsequent report in December, 1977, in which the basic dietary recommendations remained essentially unchanged from the first report. Credit must be given to the Committee for this. The new report was also improved by including sections on alcoholism and obesity.

However, in the latter report the Committee included considerable data presenting the food industry's side of the controversy. Although this would appear at first glance to have strengthened the value of the report, it does leave the uninitiated with more questions than ever. The average individual isn't aware of the voluminous research sponsored by the food industry. The sad fact is that **research is tainted by the sources of monetary support.**

## The seven conditions of health

We must believe that "we eat to live" rather than "we live to eat." Our way of eating and drinking should take into consideration the fact that our bodies are magnificent temples which will respond to our daily needs in a way unparalleled provided we care for **its** needs.

Our way of eating should result in our achieving George Ohsawa's seven conditions of health: no fatigue, good appetite, deep and good sleep, good memory, good humor, clarity in thinking and doing, and the mood of justice.

We are the creator of our own life, health, and happiness, and we must now assume this responsibility rather than relying on others.

## The macrobiotic principle applied to food selection

In Chapter 6 we discussed how our solar system depends upon a fine balancing of the opposing centripetal and centrifugal forces. In the macrobiotic terminology the centripetal constrictive force is *Yang,* the centrifugal expansive force, *Yin. Yang* is considered the male force, *Yin,* the female.

According to the macrobiotic philosophy everything on earth is influenced by these forces, plant and animal life especially. If a plant were to be influenced by more of one force, it would transmit that same force to the individual consuming it.

If an individual were to eat more *yang* foods, he would tend to be more compact, produce more heat, have a tendency toward anger, and be aggressive. If a person were to eat more *yin* foods, he would tend to be less compact, produce less heat, have a tendency toward conciliation, and be less aggressive and more passive. If you were to desire to maintain a middle road, a balance, you would want to select a diet and eat more foods close to the middle where the forces are balanced.

Michel Abehsera, a student of George Ohsawa, wrote in *Zen Macrobiotic Cooking*:

> *Yin = Acidity = Potassium = Sugar = Fruits, etc.*
> *Yang = Alkalinity = Sodium = Salt = Cereals, etc.*
> *Yin expands; sugar is yin. Sugar, when placed on the tongue, tends to make it expand.*
> *Yang contracts: Salt is yang. Salt, when placed on the tonque, tends to make it contract.*
> *If any element affects the mouth, it invariably affects the body, which in turn affects the mind. What are commonly known as drugs can be taken generally as an extreme example of yin. Drugs, extremely acid, expand the mind, diffuse concentration, cloud sensibility, etc. Excessive eating and drinking by a longer yet equally efficient process bring about the same results. Yet do not be mislead into thinking that acidity is bad! Acidity and alkalinity are necessary complementary opposites, good or bad in direct relation to quantity and balance.*
>
> *In food, the perfect balance of alkalinity and acidity is found in only one grain – brown rice. Experts, such as Dr. Rene Dubos, the Nobel prize winner, tell us that we can possibly live on this cereal alone. It contains a balance of 5 parts potassium (yin) to 1 part sodium (yang). Thus, in eating other foods, it seems that if we adhere to this ratio of 5 to 1, we are in good hands.*

My purpose is not to confuse you by attempting to describe fully the macrobiotic philosophy as it applies to food selection. These principles may appear remote and alien, even ridiculous to you. However, if you examine the theory closely, you will discover that such nutritionally bad foods as sugar, (extremely yin), and eggs and salt (dangerously yang) are forbidden macrobiotically.

For further details, the reader is referred to such books as *Zen Macrobiotic Cooking* by Michel Abehsera or to our forthcoming book describing our Center's diet. Suffice it to say, it has been our experience and that of many competent scientists that the macrobiotic principles have validity.

## Toxic foods

In our opinion, there are certain foods which should never be eaten. These are refined sugar, white flour, polished rice, red meat (beef and pork), butter, other animal fats, coffee, and tea (except herb teas). Avoid completely industrialized food and drink such as sugared soft drinks, dyed foods, all canned and bottled foods, etc. Limit your salt intake.

**Refined sugar.** Every reader interested in his own health should read William Dufty's book, *Sugar Blues.* The book is summarized in his definition of 3 words:

> **Sugar** — *refined sucrose, $C_{12}H_{22}O_{11}$, produced by multiple chemical processing of the juice of the sugar cane or beet and removal of all fiber and protein, which amount to 90% of the natural plant;* **Blues** — *a state of depression or melancholy overlaid with fear, physical discomfort, and anxiety (often expressed lyrically as an autobiographical chronicle of personal disaster);* **Sugar Blues** — *Multiple physical and mental miseries caused by human consumption of refined sucrose — commonly called sugar.*

You want to hear more? Read Mr. Dufty's eloquent #1 health best seller and get educated.

Some of the most common diseases are caused by refined sugar. Experimental studies demonstrate that rats with a genetic predisposition to diabetes will develop the disease when exposed to high sugar diets, and yet the disease can be prevented with a sugar-free diet. Epidemiological studies reveal that Yemenite Jewish immigrants to Israel had a low incidence of diabetes until they had consumed a Westernized diet high in sugar for several years.

Sugar has been implicated in tooth decay, which may be the most widespread disease related to nutrition.

Dr. John Yudkin has implicated sugar in cardiovascular disease. However, this is disputed by others.

Many suffer from hypoglycemia, low blood sugar. This condition causes one to experience weakness, headaches, and even convulsions in its severe state. Many individuals think that low blood sugar should be treated by ingesting more sugar. In fact, the opposite is true: eating sugar only temporarily raises your blood sugar, followed by a rapid drop in blood sugar, especially in the individual prone to hypoglycemia attacks. The treatment for such a condition is to eat protein and complex carbohydrates and to avoid sugar.

One of the most immediate problems often cited by nutritionists is the danger that increased sugar intake displaces complex carbohydrates which are high in micro-nutrients. The noted nutritionist, Dr. Jean Mayer states that sugar calories may acutally increase the body's needs for certain vitamins, such as thiamine and trace minerals, such as chromium. He concludes: "thus a greater burden is placed on the other components of the diet to contribute all the necessary nutrients — other foods need to show extraordinary 'nutrient density' to compensate for the emptiness of the sugar calories."

Sugar is described as "empty calories" because it lacks vitamins, minerals, or fiber. As a result the human body depletes its own store of minerals and coenzymes in order to metabolize sugar properly.

The average Westerner eats 120 pounds of refined sugar per year, or almost 25% of the total calories. The U.S. public consumes 11 million tons of sugar per year, roughly half of which is imported from the Dominican Republic, the Phillipines, Mexico and other cane producers. The other half is grown at home as beet sugar (75% from the Northwestern states) and cane sugar (25%) from Texas. The increased use of sugar is traceable in large part to the desire of food manufacturers to create unique food products with a competitive edge: for example, Nabisco's Oreo cookie with double the amount of sugar filling, and addition of sugar to cereal in 1948 to recover slumping cereal sales. Today, we find sugar not only in cold cereals, baked goods and snack foods, but also in such foods as canned vegetables, canned fish, baby foods, soups, and even in prepared meats such as bologna, hot dogs, etc. The tremendous increase in sugar usage is directly related to refined sugar being added to processed foods. The U.S. Department of Agriculture's 1971 figures show that 70% of the sugar we consume is in food products and beverages — not directly under the control of the consumer, although the consumer always has the choice of not buying and eating it.

Like salt, our desire for sugar is not a physiological necessity but an acquired taste. Dr. Yudkin found that sugar consumption not only causes an increase in blood sugar levels, but also results in a sharp rise in adrenalin, the "fight-or-flight" hormone, which may explain why sugar gives such a rush in energy, or such a fidgety feeling. Sugar addiction, and an addiction is what it is, may have its origin in the biochemistry of this hormonal joyride. This effect is worse when sugar is fed to children.

In *Dietary Goals for the United States,* the Senate's Select Committee on Nutrition and Human Needs recommends that sugar consumption be reduced by about 40% to account for about 15% of total energy intake. We at The GOTACH Center for Health believe this is even far too much. Refined sugar has **absolutely** no reason to be in our diet. It does no good. In fact, it causes only ill health conditions. Eliminate refined sugar completely from your diet and enjoy the benefits of natural carbohydrates and sugar substances.

**White flour.** Industry has taken an almost perfect grain, wheat, and stripped it of its outer coat consisting of the bran layers and the germ. The almost pure starch which remains is then bleached with sodium hypoclorite, the identical chemical from which Clorox is made. The bran gives bulk to our diet, the lack of which results in many gastrointestinal dis-ease states and possibly contributes to the development of cancer. The germ contains many needed vitamins, including the B-complex which man usually must obtain from meat.

It makes no sense to take a perfect grain, strip it of its most important ingredients, and then eat the chemicalized "empty calories" remaining. Man then compounds his error by fortifying the white flour with the addition of iron, other minerals, and vitamins, in proportions not contained in the original grain. Man still has not learned that within Nature there is a perfect wisdom. Everytime man alters this design he discovers that he has made a mistake!

Learn to eat bread made with freshly ground whole wheat flour because many components of the germ layer are destroyed from exposure to oxygen. We know that the body metabolizes and acts differently after consuming native unaltered carbohydrates as contrasted to eating the same amount of purified starch in the form of white flour and polished rice.

Wheat is not the most perfect food, however. There are many individuals who have a sensitivity to wheat glutein which is not removed by stripping and bleaching. These individuals must avoid eating wheat and wheat products in order to stay healthy. You can determine your sensitivity to wheat by eliminating wheat from your diet for 6 weeks and determine whether there is a difference in how you feel before and after.

**Polished rice.** Man has committed similar crimes with rice, which is considered by many to be the perfect food. Allergic sensitivity to rice is extremely rare. I do not know of any case, although I would assume that there may exist a few individuals in the world who cannot tolerate rice. In health and medicine there are few absolutes!

Man again stripped the bran- and germ-containing outer coat and fed the "empty calories" of the remaining pure starch to the masses. This custom goes back to the times of Confucius who advocated polishing rice. He might have had indigestion the day he made that promulgation!

We now know that the outer coat of the rice kernel contains considerable protein, fat, many minerals and vitamins. Almost all of the B-complex vitamins, including B-12, are contained in the outer rice coat which is unwisely discarded in processing.

Begin eating brown rice, especially the short grain variety. It is truly an almost perfect food in the natural state.

**Red meat.** The population of the United States and the Western world allegedly eats too much red meat in the form of beef and pork. It is almost impossible to keep your saturated fat intake down to where it should be for optimum health if you eat beef. Almost 75 percent of the calories of the leanest piece of filet mignon are from saturated fat — fat which you cannot see because it is microscopically "marbled" between the individual muscle fibers. This is the reason why beef tastes so good.

Most of the taste of meats and other foods come from fats. With chicken the fat is in the outer skin, and it has been determined that people who eat a lot of plain chicken get the "chicken blahs." You have to do something to make chicken tasty — bread it, coat it with herbs and spices, pour barbecue sauce over it, etc. This is because unlike beef, chicken does not have fat between the microscopic muscle fibers.

In addition, eating red meat causes you to be aggressive. If you don't believe me stop eating red meat for 30 days and observe what happens to your psyche and emotional state. You will become more peaceful and tolerant, and you will notice that you will not react as much to outside negative challenges. You will begin to handle situations better. Not only have I experienced these changes but almost all of those I have known who discontinued eating red meat have had similar experiences. I urge you **not** to believe me. Try it and experience it for yourself.

If you have a cardiac condition, avoiding red meat completely may be life-promoting, if not life-saving. The long term consumption of red meat consumption with its high levels of saturated fat is one of the major causes of heart dis-ease.

**Butter and other animal fats.** The reason for eliminating fat in the diet is to make a place for complex carbohydrates which carry higher levels of micro-nutrients than fat, without the complications of fat.

If you exercise a lot or actively engage in a sport (i.e. marathon runner) you may need more fat in your diet (Chapter 11). But for the ordinary individual who does not exercise a lot, eating too many fats will result in obesity and other dis-ease states.

**Salt.** Although salt is necessary for life, excessive intake should be avoided.

All living cells must maintain a specific salt concentration for proper functioning. When the cellular salt concentration is significantly altered dis-ease states ensue. Low concentrations of sodium resulting from severe diarrhea, excessive perspiration, etc. will cause you to get headaches and eventually may lead to coma, convulsions and death. "Sun stroke" is not directly caused by overexposure to the sun, but rather from excessive loss of salt from heat and perspiration. The salt concentration may be further lowered when the individual drinks water to quench his thirst. In order to prevent losses of sodium you must replace the salt by either taking salt pills or drinking fluids containing salt, such as Gatorade.

Excessive salt intake results in disturbances of body functions. Acute salt poisoning caused by accidental ingestion can result in coma and death. Chronic intake of too much salt causes our body to retain excessive salt. In an attempt to regulate and maintain a normal concentration, the body retains water. This results in the system having too much fluid. Blood pressure increases and the heart is overworked. Long standing high blood pressure can result in permanent alteration of the vessels in the eyes, kidneys, and elsewhere in the body.

Refined **table salt** is 99.99% sodium chloride, or NaCl, no matter where it originally came from: the salt spring near Onondaga, New York; the sea salt factories around the San Francisco Bay; the salt mines in Texas, Louisiana, and beneath the city of Detroit. Some of these sources contain nearly 100% pure NaCl in the natural state. Others have small amounts of other salt minerals which are essentially all removed by the refining process. **Rock salt** comes from deposits which were formed when shifts in the earth's crust buried parts of the sea millions of years ago. Although these deposits initially contained non-NaCl minerals, eons of rainfall have leached these from the rock salt deposits and washed them into the sea. **Sea salt** contains not only other non-NaCl minerals such as potassium (K), calcium (Ca), magnesium (Mg) but also the so called "trace elements," such as silicon (Si), copper (Cu), nickel (Ni), manganese (Mn), etc. Because the body requires all these minerals, we recommend using sea salt, as nature had originally intended.

There is one very important element in sea salt that the body requires but which is lost in processing. Iodine, which is essential to the formation of thyroid hormones, is very volatile and destroyed when exposed to light. Iodized salt has potassium iodide added to it to provide the **antigoiter** factor. Dextrose, a simple sugar, must then be added to stabilize the iodine so it will not volatilize and be destroyed by light. Sodium bicarbonate is added to bleach out the purple color caused by the potassium iodide and dextrose. And finally, sodium silico-aluminate is added to coat the crystals so that the salt will be free-flowing in humid weather. Natural salts are not free-flowing. They will naturally attract moisture from the air.

Let's consider for a moment what technology has done for us. Processing has refined out the non-NaCl minerals and trace elements the body needs for its proper metabolism. Then it is bleached, and sugar and drying chemicals are added. Because the salt is free-flowing it is easier for us to unconsciously pour excessive amounts of this substance on our food. This can contribute to a possible imbalance in the body and eventually to ill health.

Our holistic philosophy maintains that we are responsible for our health. Therefore, we should develop good health-habits that restore our body to what nature originally intended. With our bodies well, our minds begin to function more clearly and we begin to experience a joy-of-living. A new spirit awakens within us.

The average adult needs considerably less salt than is our custom and habit of consuming. Salt consumption in the United States is estimated to range from about 6 to 18 grams a day, according to the National Academy of Sciences' 1974 publication, *Recommended Dietary Allowances.* In *Dietary Goals for the United States,* the U.S. Senate's Select Committee on Nutrition and Human Needs has recommended that salt consumption be reduced by about 50 to 85% to 3 grams/day. This allowance was derived from the Academy's report. Drs. George Meneely and Harold Battarbee, in *Present Knowledge in Nutrition,* suggest that the average human requirement for salt is probabaly only about half a gram and can normally be achieved without adding salt to the food. They further state that desire for salt is not a physiological necessity but rather an acquired taste.

Adequate amounts of salt can be extracted from the foods we eat. All plant- and animal-derived foods contain salt minerals which can be extracted by the body according to its needs. When thinking about your needs for added salt, consider your diet, water intake, physical activity, and the climate. If you are sedentary you will require less salt than if you are physically active and perspire a great deal.

Eat a balanced diet and you will develop better nutritional balance. The iodine your body requires can be extracted from sea foods such as fish and sea vegetables. Although sea vegetables as purchased in natural food stores are dried, the iodine contained therein is stabilized by the natural complex sugars in the plants' leaves. Most sea vegetables contain 4-8% salt; they can be roasted and ground up and used in place of salt.

Rather than indiscriminately pouring excessive amounts of refined, free-flowing salt upon your food, develop the habit of using salt-containing condiments such as sesame salt. You will enjoy the added taste, but, more importantly, you will use less salt. There is considerable evidence to show that eating foods as close to their natural state does provide the body with the nutrients needed for a healthy life. And eating these natural foods can be an enjoyable experience.

**Coffee and other stimulating drinks.** Much of an individual's inability to cope with stress can be related to the consumption of coffee, tea and other stimulating drinks. It must be remembered that substances which allegedly over-stimulate your brain, central nervous system, and mind will cause you to be nervous and uptight. High on the list of such chemicals is caffeine.

Coffee which contains the highest amount of caffeine is, of course, the greatest culprit—one cup of coffee has 90 to 125 milligrams (mg). Coffee is consumed by many young and middle aged adults, a group very much affected by stress. Tea contains 30-70 mg.

Have you ever wondered how much caffeine is found in various soft drinks. Recent studies reveal the following: Coca-Cola, 64.7 mg; Dr. Pepper, 60.9 mg; Mountain Dew, 54.7 mg; Diet Dr. Pepper, 54.2 mg; Tab, 49.4 mg; Pepsi, 43.1 mg; R C Cola, 33.7 mg; Diet R C, 33 mg; Diet Rite, 31.7 mg. Most parents who wouldn't give their children coffee because of the caffeine, think nothing of giving them amounts of soft drinks which contain more caffeine than a normal adult consumes from coffee and tea. This may account for a child who is cranky, hard to please, has a behavior problem or may be experiencing difficulty in concentrating, having learning problems, or who is hyperactive. If your child has difficulty sleeping or is a bed wetter, these behaviors can also be related to caffeine.

The adult who consumes 5 to 8 cups of coffee per day is asking for coping problems. He is unable to calm down enough to take his challenges in stride, unable to relax, unable to get a good night's sleep.

I'm always asked: "What about decaffeinated coffee?" That's probably worse! Decaffeinated coffee might seem like a good option for coffee lovers who want to avoid caffeine. Unfortunately, there are two health hazards as consequences.

First the chemical solvent that almost every decaffeinating plant uses today to leach the caffeine from the green coffee beans is *methylenechloride*. This substance, which is in the same chemical family of chlorinated hydrocarbons as dry-cleaning fluids, is currently under suspicion as a cancer-inducing agent. The National Cancer Institute is currently investigating the effects of inhaling and ingesting methylenechloride. However, the results of these tests are not yet available. In the meantime, the FDA has placed a maximum level of permissible solvent residue in roasted decaffeinated beans at 10 parts per million, a figure many sources still consider risky. Second, the decaffeinating process introduces an amount of nickel that many consider toxic and dangerous.

There is a lesson here: the chemical alteration of foods usually results in chemical residuals which in themselves may increase the toxicity of the food.

Consider eliminating the habit of drinking coffee, tea (except herb teas), cola-containing and other soft drinks. You will notice a calming effect as a result. Avoid offering these drinks to your children. Teach them good health habits now so that they may enjoy living.

**Chemical food additives.** Although I am discussing only a few of the toxic foods, I would be remiss if I didn't mention something about chemical food additives.

Modern technology is responsible for the production of tremendous quantities of food to feed the population masses. Never before in history have we had the know how and capability of virtually eliminating hunger from the world. Unfortunately, this technology is not being used wisely. More than ever industry is using chemical food additives as colors, flavors, preservatives, thickeners and other substances for controlling the physical properties of food. There are more than 1,300 food additives currently approved for use in the U.S., and the exact amounts being used are unknown.

The Food and Drug Administration in 1976 estimated that the average daily consumption of artificial colors alone among children aged 1 to 5 may be about 75 milligrams. The largest single category contributing to artificial coloring consumption among children was beverages. More accurate measures may be available after the FDA completes its 1977 survey.

The FDA bases its consideration of the safety of chemical food additives upon varying degrees of testing, review of scientific literature, expert opinion and longtime usage. The most testing has involved animal toxicity studies with artificial colors. Artificial flavors have been tested the least. In 1977, the FDA begun a re-evaluation of the safety of colors, flavors and direct additives.

What information can animal studies provide? Varying degrees and quality of animal testing may provide useful data on the effects of chemical additives on the animal systems employed, but how can these results be related to man? Our life span is approaching ¾ of a century and the effects of chemical additives consumed as a child might not become evident for 20 to 60 years. There are continuing discoveries of apparent connections between certain additives and cancer, and possibly hyperactivity. This gives justifiable cause to seek to reduce additive consumption to the greatest degree possible. There are increasing numbers of knowledgeable and concerned scientists in this field who advocate that only those additives that serve a necessary function should be permitted in food. What is necessary is defined as that which is needed to insure food safety.

Ruth Fremes and Zak Sabru in their publication *Nutri Score* have classified as unnecessary and possibly a hazard to health several additives commonly considered under the heading of preservatives and flavor enhancers, e.g., nitrates and nitrites; BHT and BHA; and monosodium glutamate. Referring to nitrates and nitrites, *Nutri Score* comments:

> While these additives are not in themselves harmful, they may combine with other chemicals in food or in the intestine to form nitrosamines, which are known to cause cancer. The advantage of using nitrites in processed foods is that they maintain a pinkish-red color, which makes the meat look fresh and attractive, and they check the growth of bacteria. Some of these bacteria, like botulinum produce deadly poisons. Government should therefore limit the addition of nitrites to the amount needed to check growth of botulinum bacteria and no more.
>
> This has been done in Canada, where the Canadian Health Protection Branch has recently reduced the amounts of nitrates and nitrites allowed in cured and processed meats. Industry, for its part, should find a preservative other than nitrite that will be effective against bacteria, yet will not present a cancer hazard. (Quoted from *Dietary Goals for the United States*, February 1977 issue, page 56).

The chemical preservatives, BHT and BHA, are not essential and there are foods on the market not employing these additives.

There is even less need for the chemical, monosodium glutamate, which is merely a flavor enhancer and not a necessary food additive. This chemical has been associated with headaches, flushes in the head and body and tingling in the spine. It is also a source of sodium and can be hazardous to individuals who must restrict their sodium intake.

Let us analyze for a moment the reasons why certain additives are employed: **Artificial colors** are employed solely to make the food pleasing to the eye. Have you wondered why so many soft drinks are colored red? It's because red emits stimulating vibrations, thus increasing the desire to drink more. The bright yellow color of butter and margarine, the deep blue color of soft drinks, the bright colors of cake frostings, etc. are all psychologically geared to get your attention and to excite you into desiring that food. Our motivation for eating should be hunger and nothing else. In my opinion, the single most important contributing factor to dis-ease in our society today is that we eat too much. Enhancing the color of food solely for the purpose of enticing us to eat more is against the principle of good health. The practice of adding chemcial coloring agents should be stopped.

**Artificial flavors** are used to enhance the way food tastes or to impart a flavor where there is little natural flavor. As we use more flavorings we suppress our taste buds. This is what happens when we constantly use salt. The same is true when we use sugar, sugar and more sugar. In fact, sugar is now being used by food manufacturers to accommodate the "sweet tooth" of the U.S. consumer. Sugar is found in canned vegetables, canned fish, baby foods, soups, and even prepared meats such as bologna, hot dogs, etc. Fortunately, the suppressive effect added flavoring has upon our taste buds is reversible. Returning to a diet rich in native grains and vegetables with some fish can enhance your tasting ability to the point where natural foods become enjoyable and pleasing to eat.

**Artificial preservatives** are employed to prevent spoilage and destroy harmful bacteria. One should remember that preservatives are poisons and anti-metabolites, that is, they destroy basic living enzyme systems. Is this what we need to take into our bodies? There are some natural methods of preserving which do not add poisons to the body. These include salting, pickling in brine, drying, freezing, refrigerating, etc. There are many foods, such as whole grains, root crops, etc. which can keep for long periods of time without spoilage provided there are proper conditions. We must be on our guard not to introduce into our bodies industrial chemicals that our cells are unable to deal with. As we become more aware of how chemicals affect our body, we will then be more careful about what we consume.

Be alert. Begin reading labels. Become an educated consumer in the market place. Protect your body from the chemical onslaught. Your health and life may depend on it.

## Schedule for meals

Since meal schedules are an individual matter which vary according to life styles, a general rule of thumb is suggested here. Let me mention a couple different schools of thought concerning breakfast—one being that since the period of sleep uses this time for the rejuvenation of the body cells, morning (or whenever the period after sleep) is the time when the body has the highest usuable energy in a 24 hour period. Therefore, a very **light** food intake, such as a serving of fresh fruit and/or fruit juice, would be in order so as not to draw from the energy level.

On the other hand, a "big" breakfast is said to fuel the body for a physically active day. An interesting point to consider is that the body's energy usually acts on priority, and, when the food enters the body, the digestive process begins to operate automatically. There is a school of thought which advises us to eat breakfast like a king, lunch like a prince, and dinner like a pauper. The average individual is most active in the morning. Eating a large breakfast will result in more calorie energy at a time when it is most needed. Evening is usually a time of decreased physical activity, and less food should probably be consumed then. Excess calorie energy produced within the body at a time when it is not being used results in storage of that energy, usually as fat.

Obviously, if an individual's life style is different, such as working a night shift, an evening performer, etc. then the time of eating and amount of food should be adjusted appropriately.

## A balanced vegetarian diet

We believe that a balanced vegetarian diet is the most natural and healthiest for man. However, we realize that many are unable at this time to make this total commitment. If you are overweight, the most important goals are to lose weight and to maintain your ideal weight thereafter. You may wish to consult your physician as to what your ideal weight should be. Most individuals instinctively know when they have arrived at their ideal weight not only by weighing on a scale, but rather by how they look stripped (or in a bathing suit if you're really shy) before a mirror!

Table 10-1 describes the percent calories in three diets; Modern American, Dietary Goals of U.S., and Nature's diets. We suggest going one step further than what is recommended by the Senate Select Committee in their *Dietary Goals of the United States.* We believe that what we call "Nature's Diet" is the most ideal. If you are suffering from a serious diet-related dis-ease and are so motivated, it would be worthwhile for you to follow this diet which is balanced to achieve body-mind-spirit unity, the holistic goal. We do not minimize the great value of the Dietary Goals Diet. If you adhere to this diet you will experience great health benefits. We do not recommend the Modern American Diet.

### Table 10-1
### PERCENT OF CALORIES IN 3 DIETS

| Food Types | Modern American Diet | | Dietary Goals of U.S. | | Nature's Diet | |
|---|---|---|---|---|---|---|
| Carbohydrate | 46* | | 58 | | 73-75 | |
|    Sugar (refined) | | 24 | | 15 | | 3-5 |
|    Complex (native) | | 22 | | 40-45 | | 70-80 |
| Protein | 12 | | 12 | | 8-12 | |
| Fat | 42 | | 30 | | 10-15 | |
|    Saturated | | 16 | | 10 | | 3 |
|    Unsaturated | | 26 | | 20 | | 7-10 |

*All figures are percentages

We are presenting a modification of our Center's Diet to help you achieve both the Dietary Goals and Nature's Diets:

1. **Overeating is the worst thing to do with respect to eating. Overeating leads to many problems such as obesity, sicknesses and inability to think clearly.**

2. **The following food items should never be eaten: sugar, white flour, polished rice, red meat, (beef and pork), butter, other animal fats, eggs, coffee and tea (except herb teas).**
   **Avoid completely industralized food and drink such as sugared soft drinks, dyed foods, all canned and bottled foods, etc.**
   **Avoid as much as possible fruits and vegetables artificially grown with chemical fertilizers and/or insecticides.**

3. **The following items should be eaten sparingly, if they must be eaten at all: white meat (chicken, turkey and lamb) milk and cheese, alcoholic beverages.**

4. **Intake of the following should be limited to once or twice weekly: fish, seafood. Shrimp should be avoided if you are really trying to reduce significantly saturated fats.**

5. **Body odor, especially under the arms, comes from eating animal foods.**

6. **The 5 causes of obesity are: sugar, unnatural starch, fat, excess protein and water. The natural starch in whole grains**

such as brown rice and whole wheat is beneficial and healthy as contrasted to the unnatural starch of white flour and polished rice.

7. One must learn to chew each mouthful at least 50 times. This is one of the most important rules of eating. You may find that when you chew slowly your hunger may be completely satisfied halfway through your meal. If you are trying to lose weight, remove your plate from before you at this time. If you have achieved your desired weight, continue to eat until you feel you have taken in sufficient nourishment.

8. Excess salt is harmful. Only sea salt should be consumed.

9. Relax and do not discuss problems while eating.

10. Fasting one day a week is good for the soul, as well as the body.

11. Remember to always bless your food before you eat it. Throughout history and in all religions we find reference to the blessing of our food at meal times. Since food is living and sensitive to all vibrations, it is important to pray and be thankful for our food. This charges our meal with positive energy removing any negativity it may have absorbed throughout its life. The food then becomes energy for the maintenance and growth of a higher form of life, the human temple.

## Fasting

Learning to cope with stress and developing self-responsibility for your life's affairs depends upon developing self-discipline over both your body and mind. Fasting is one of the best ways of achieving this goal.

In many civilizations throughout history reference is made to fasting as a vehicle for man to strengthen his spirituality. Fasting lets the body know who is boss, because it establishes the mind and spirit as superior forces not to be easily influenced by bodily desires.

Although man derives much pleasure from his physical senses, overdoing it may actually deaden the experience. It is a well established fact, for instance, that the more salt or sugar you use to season your food, the more you will require to experience an equivalent degree of the particular taste. This is why individuals develop the habit of adding more and more salt or sugar. This is what leads to addiction not only to certain food substances but also to drugs and medications.

If, on the other hand, you were to stop eating salt or sugar completely for several weeks, the taste buds would regenerate and become much more sensitive to small amounts of flavoring substances.

In my opinion, this is the same situation with overeating. This is a habit which develops from a lack of self-discipline about eating. We accept the fact that eating is a pleasurable event. It is meant to be so. An overeater usually bolts his food down without chewing it well. He doesn't satisfy his hunger nor his eating senses enough so that he must eat more to achieve the pleausre he desires. As a result of overeating, he becomes obese, which, as mentioned earlier, further aggravates his self-image.

**Self-discipline is the key to controlling not only your physical senses but also your whole life.** Self-discipline is not abusing and torturing yourself. Self-mutilation is not and should not be one of our aims. Self-discipline is rather the state you are in when your body, mind, and spirit are finely tuned to each other with the mind and spirit in control. When you have achieved this state you experience joy and happiness.

Have you ever watched a spoiled child or an untrained animal? It is possible they have a lot in common! The spoiled child is never satisfied. The more you give him, the more he wants. He is always manipulating others to get his way, and, when he does, he still is not happy. He is usually grumpy all the time. An untrained animal is much the same way—never relaxed, uptight, constantly seeking attention, etc.

A well trained animal is usually a happy one. Watch as they perform with their head held high, proud of themselves, and if they could smile you would be able to see that too. Well disciplined children are also happy. They are proud of themselves and derive a great deal of satisfaction from their accomplishments.

We have digressed a bit here, but, the point is that fasting is an excellent exercise to develop self-discipline.

How does one fast? You don't need to go on a 40 day fast, although this has been done by One to achieve mastery over His carnal desires! Select a day of the week and instead of eating your usual meals, drink a glass of water or fruit juice for breakfast, eat a small cup of brown rice for lunch, and a bowl of soup for dinner or supper. Double your exercise for that day. I will guarantee that not only on that day, but on the following day also, you will experience a fantastic emotional high. You will experience the feeling that you can do anything and everything. Try it. If you have any medical condition consult your physician to insure that fasting is not contraindicated.

You will begin to experience your negative emotions of fear, anger and hatred being replaced by the positive emotions of love, tolerance, and joy. Negative emotions are the result of being out of control and lacking self-discipline. Much of the stress individuals experience comes from an unstable emotional state. Learning to be in control achieves mastery over your emotions. You are then well on your way toward controlling stress in your life.

# CHAPTER 11

# HOW PHYSICAL EXERCISE AFFECTS STRESS

## General comments about metabolism

Exercise affects our physical, mental, emotional, and spiritual health and our ability to cope with stress. Here are some basic facts about how our bodies metabolize food. Metabolism is essentially the process by which food is converted into body-building protein, bio-chemicals (i.e., hormones, vitamins, enzymes, etc.), and energy.

Proper diet insures that we consume the vitamins and minerals the body is unable to manufacture. There are also the essential amino-acids, the building blocks of protein which the body cannot make and, therefore must be provided by the diet. The body is able to manufacture most of the amino acids (except the "essential" ones), fatty acids, and hormones. However, it requires energy to do so. Although proteins can be converted into energy, most of the energy is derived from two major food sources: carbohydrates and fats.

Energy within living systems is measured in calories, which is defined as the amount of heat energy required to raise the temperature of one gram of water one degree centigrade. Carbohydrates and proteins contain 4 calories per gram and fats 8 calories per gram. One can readily appreciate that fats contain twice the calorie energy than carbohydrates and proteins.

Since carbohydrates and fats are the major sources of energy, a discussion of how they are metabolized is appropriate. Carbohydrates, which should make up the major portion of our food energy can be metabolized in one of two ways (Table 11-1), either aerobically (a system requiring oxygen) or anaerobically (not requiring oxygen). Fats can **only** be metabolized aerobically.

Keep in mind that the body is a great conservationist. It will and does conserve the excess energy it produces by converting it either

107

**Table 11-1**
**EFFECT OF OXYGEN ON METABOLISM**

| Food Source | Oxygen Requirements (aerobic or anaerobic) | Product of Metabolism | Excess Energy |
|---|---|---|---|
| Carbohydrates (complex and simple sugars) | requires Oxygen (aerobic) → | Energy | excess energy reconverted and stored as glycogen and FAT |
| | no Oxygen required (anaerobic) → | Energy | |
| Fats | requires Oxygen (aerobic) → | Energy | |

into glycogen, a complex animal carbohydrate, which can be readily reconverted to simple sugars for quick metabolism, or into fat, which usually gets stored in conspicuous places around the body and which is not readily reconverted to energy.

## Aerobic vs. anaerobic exercise programs

As can be readily surmised from Table 11-1, aerobic exercise is preferred to anaerobic, especially if you have a tendency toward being overweight and fat.

Being fat and overweight can not only be the result of your inability to cope with stress, but it may also be the stressful condition causing you to be unhappy. Although the answer to the obesity problem may be simple, developing the self-discipline to carry out the solution may be more difficult.

The answer to weight control cannot be found completely in diet without exercise. How many diets have you or your friends tried? Maybe you've tried the Atkins or Stillmans high protein, low-carbohydrate diet. You may have tried the juice diet, the drinking man's diet, the "L-C" low-carbohydrate diet, the liquid proline diet, the rice diet, the juice diet, the starvation diet, and many others. Maybe you've experienced what most fat people experience: that you initially lose weight on any diet you try, but that you eventually level off and further weight loss is impossible. You may eventually gain weight on less than a 1000 calorie diet.

Let me reassure you. You're not a freak! What you experience can be scientifically explained. The first rule is that the average fat person cannot achieve permanent weight loss and control by diet alone. I don't care what any of the authors of diet books say, what weight watchers preach or what the Fat Farms tell you. Isn't it interesting that fat people keep on visiting their Gurus at the Fat Farms. This is because they very seldom experience a permanent cure. The second rule is that you must regularly exercise **aerobically** in order to lose weight and keep it off. Let me explain why this is so.

Muscle tissue makes up a large portion of the body: about 40% in a male who is in reasonably good shape; about 32% in the female. In addition, muscle is a highly metabolic tissue. It takes many more calories for our muscles to operate than it takes for the brain or many other organs to function. The muscle tissue in the body burns up about 90 percent of what you eat. It utilizes 90 percent of those calories and 90 percent of the vitamins and minerals you consume.

It may surprise you to know that a high-protein/low-carbohydrate diet is a **muscle losing diet.** The body needs carbohydrates in the form of simple sugars, such as glucose, to operate. When it doesn't get enough, it will make its own by a process called *gluconeogenesis.* This term essentially means to *make new sugar.* And, the body does this by breaking down the body's own protein, usually in the muscle, and converting it into glucose. You may not realize that when you lose 25 pounds on this type of diet, although 15 of those pounds may be fat, the other 10 pounds may be muscle. It is possible that several of these pounds may be water, but at least 5 to 7 of the pounds is muscle.

Everytime you go on a diet which causes you to lose muscle, at the end of the diet, there is less of you to burn up what you eat. Thus you get fatter more quickly the second time than you did the first time. The sad thing about most fat people who lose weight is that they usually regain what they lose **plus 5 pounds more**! Do something permanent for yourself. You cannot go on a diet which causes you to lose the very tissue you need not to be fat. Watch your calories, be smart, and exercise to increase the muscle mass of your body so that you become a larger calorie burning individual.

There are added benefits you can derive from a regular aerobic exercise program. The body adapts to the conditions you place before it. If you exercise aerobically, 20 to 30 minutes three times per week, the enzymes controlling aerobic metabolism will double in amount in 6 months time. You will then become more efficient in your aerobic metabolism and in your fat-burning capabilities.

## An aerobic exercise formula

You're probably wondering what the aerobic forms of exercise are and how can they be distinguished from anerobic forms? It is difficult to classify exercises as being all aerobic or all anaerobic because this depends upon how the exercise is performed. For instance jogging can be aerobic: while you are jogging your metabolism rate is sufficiently raised without you losing your breath. When you've reached the point where you are out of breath, you become relatively oxygen starved and you are in an anaerobic phase. Jogging, bicycling, swimming, dancing, and brisk walking (while moving your hands, arms and torso), are excellent forms of aerobic exercise because the rate of exercise can be controlled to keep you in the aerobic phase. Football, basketball, tennis, raquet ball, hockey, etc., are mainly anaerobic. The nature of these sports is such that you are unable to control and maintain a steady exercise rate: you are in an anaerobic phase while you're moving fast and out of breath and in an inefficient metabolic phase while you're slowing down. Bicycling which is controlled on level ground can be aerobic, but it becomes anaerobic when the course consists of hills. You're most likely anaerobic going up the hill and in an inefficient metabolic phase coming down the hill. The same is true of running up and down stairs.

Our advice is to select a form of exercise which you can control and perform regularly, daily or at least three days per week, 20 to 30 minutes each time.

A simple formula which you can use to indicate when you are in the aerobic phase is:

(200 - your age) - 10% of (200 - your age) = the heart rate you should maintain to be in the aerobic phase.

For a 30 year old individual this would be:

(200-30) - 10% (200-30) = heart rate
    170  -      17        = 153

For a 40 year old individual this would be:

(200-40) - 10% (200-40) = heart rate
    160  -      16        = 144

For a 60 year old individual it would be:

(200-60) - 10% (200-60) = heart rate
    140  -      14        = 126

Provided there are no adverse symptoms such as chest pain, dizzy spells, etc. this is a fairly safe formula. If you have a history of heart dis-ease or tuberculosis consult your physician as to the advisability of this type of exercising. The only condition of which I am aware where any form of exercise is **absolutely** contra-indicated and should not be performed is tuberculosis. With other conditions, even moderately severe heart dis-ease, there is a safe margin. In fact, with coronary heart disease regular exercise is a must for rehabilitation.

## Posture

One aspect of physical exercise which is frequently ignored is *posture*. Watch the average person walking down the street — head and shoulders slouched and the rest of the body not in line with the body's center of gravity. Observe as he sits in a chair — again with slouched head and neck and with curved spine. There is little wonder that people experience so much tension in the head, neck and upper shoulders area, and so much low back pain.

Slovenly posture causes tremendous strain on muscles, ligaments, tendons, bones, and nerves. Because it is usually constant and long-term, it results in atrophy and the subsequent loss of strength of the muscles. This is the prime cause of low back pain. The muscles of the lower back are some of the smaller muscles of the body. These muscles do not need to be any larger for they are more than adequate to do the job they were supposed to do if correct posture is maintained.

In the slouched posture the body is hanging because gravity tends to pull the body down to the ground. Consequently, the anti-gravity muscles, those involved with keeping the body erect, are in a constant state of tension — an inefficient state of muscle function. There is an accumulation within the muscles of lactic acid, a product of anaerobic glucose metabolism causing muscle fatigue. Eventually the muscle goes into spasm, a condition causing pain in the affected area.

If you were to maintain a correct posture, one which would insure that your body is in line with the center of gravity, that is, the head and neck up, shoulders back, and spine straight, you would use both opposing muscle groups, the gravity (flexor) and anti-gravity (extensor), to regulate this balance. Both muscles would develop equally without imbalance and strain. You can use the center of gravity to maintain your body in an erect position much more efficiently than if you were to fight gravity constantly.

Individuals who purchase very comfortable contoured chairs are pampering their lower back muscles causing them to further atrophy (get smaller and lose strength). They are setting themselves up for low back muscle spasm problems.

Develop a calisthenic exercise program designed to strengthen the muscles of the neck and back. All you really need to do is stand up erect and sit up straight in a manner lining your whole body up along your center of gravity line. You will experience a sense of physical well being and prevent some of the causes of head, neck, shoulder, and low back fatigue and pain experienced so much by modern day man.

Yoga, one of the meditation/exercises is a very good discipline designed to stretch your tendons, strengthen your muscles, maintain an erect "disciplined" posture, and, at the same time, relax your body and mind. Seek out an individual who regularly practices yoga and observe how relaxed and "laid back" his personality is. He's not experiencing difficulty coping with stress (Chapter 12)!

## Breathing

Another aspect of physical exercise to consider is breathing. Under normal non-exerting situations, the average individual uses only about 30 percent of his lung capacity to breathe. The lower third of his lung very seldom gets inflated. Anytime a portion of the body is not being used sufficiently, tissue fluids accumulate in the area. As a result of inefficient use of the lower portions of the lung, tissue fluids build up to cause congestion. The next time that individual is exposed to an upper respiratory pathogen, he becomes a prime target for that micro-organism to settle in the congested area and multiply. Dis-ease then ensues.

Another condition resulting from poor breathing practices is the development of weakened diaphragm. From this, hiatus hernias can develop — a condition where abdominal organs, such as the stomach, herniate through the diaphragm into the chest cavity. This can be a most uncomfortable and painful dis-ease situation.

Efficient breathing involves using the diaphragm to pull air into the deeper areas of the lung bases, using the intercostal (between the ribs) muscles to draw air into the upper portions, and exhaling in reverse order, the upper lung followed by the lower lung areas. When controlled, this type of breathing refreshes and energizes both the body and mind. It is employed in yoga and should be a part of your meditation exercises.

As a result of regular controlled diaphragmatic breathing you will also experience less upper respiratory and pulmonary infections. You will enjoy improved health and more easily maintain that state of wellness we all desire.

## Rest and recreation

Set aside time for rest and recreation daily. Definitely include rest as part of any exercise program: yoga, aikido, aerobics, calisthenics, etc. It is a time for the body to relax and for the mind to enter an altered state of consciousness. Rest and relaxation are integral parts of meditation in as much as prior to entering the meditative state you relax the muscles of your body to allow you to enter deeper levels of your mind.

You may be unaware that this situation occurs frequently and naturally during the course of living. You may remember the time you were working in the yard or doing some other chore around the house or office and you felt fatigued. You took a short break, maybe a cool drink, and sat in a chair for about five minutes or so. You dozed off or possibly daydreamed for a moment. Then you awoke from this semi-reverie state and remarked to yourself that you were refreshed — that you got your "second wind." What actually happened was that, when you sat down and relaxed, you entered an altered state of consciousness (while day dreaming you're producing ALPHA brain waves). You experienced an increase in mental energy. Nature has provided man with the ability to self-generate his own energy. Rest and relaxation provides the opportunity to activate this capacity.

Recreation is also very important. "All work and no play makes Jack a dull boy!" Remember that it does the same for Jane! Oftentimes we are so close to a challenge that we lose perspective. We can't see the forest because we're concentrating too much on a single tree.

Take time to stand back so that you can see the "big picture." Get involved in some form of enjoyable recreation. Take your mind away from the challenge and get involved in some play situation. Frequently the challenge will diminish, sometimes it will disappear. Remember that one of man's difficulties is that he attempts to solve a problem at the level of the problem. *The solution always lies at a level above the problem.* You must achieve a level of consciousness above that you were in when the challenge arose. When you have arrived at the solution of a problem, you have succeeded in reaching a higher level of consciousness.

Recreation allows you the opportunity to refresh your mind so that when you return to your challenge you can view it from a broader perspective. You are afforded the chance to grow in understanding.

## Recommended exercises

I am not going to recommend any particular form of exercise other than what I've already said—that the best exercises are aerobic.

However, I do advise that you choose a form of physical exercise you enjoy. You may enjoy jogging, hiking, swimming, bicycle riding, calisthenics (from the Greek, *kallos,* beauty plus *stenos,* strength), horseback riding, etc. Select a form of aerobic exercise you enjoy. Do not employ a form you don't enjoy, just for the sake of exercising. Exercise is not just for the body. It is also for the mind. If a form of exercise is a chore, your mind does not get relaxed. In fact, it may tend to get more uptight.

Include a program of planned physical aerobic exercise or a form of meditative/exercise (e.g. yoga, aikido, etc.), which you enjoy, as a part of your physical, mental, and spiritual health endeavors.

## The effect of exercise upon physical, mental, emotional and spiritual health

Physical exercise teaches the body the correct way to go. The efficiency of your cardiovascular system improves. Your heart increases in size, resting heart rate decreases, and the ability of your heart to function as an efficient pumping system improves. As a result your blood pressure usually decreases and stabilizes. All the tissues and organs of your body receive more oxygen and you experience physical vigor and strength, clarity of thinking, and better overall health.

Lack of exercise results in anerobic metabolism and a build up of lactic acid in the muscles. This lactic acid build up is the cause of muscle fatigue. When your metabolism is mostly aerobic, lactic acid is not produced and your muscles do not experience true fatigue. This is the reason why long distance marathon runners seem to go on and on!

Frank Shorter, the Olympic marathon runner, eats approximately 5,000 calories per day. He is a healthy specimen of mankind with a resting heart rate of 52. His other cardiovascular parameters also reflect excellent body function. He can and must consume large amounts of calories because of aerobic exercise.

It is now well known that joggers experience what is being called the *joggers' high.* This is being explained on the basis of *endorphin* production. Several investigators have injected morphine- and endorphin- antagonists into runners after jogging. Following this injection, the joggers experience a tremendous psychological let down. Further research is needed to further explain this phenomenon.

Anyone who regularly exercises admits to experiencing increased clarity of thinking following exercise. This most likely can be explained by increased oxygen supply to the brain, decreased lactic acid accumulation in the muscles, and *endorphin* production. The brain is very sensitive to oxygen. A lack of oxygen to the brain for 3 to 5 minutes usually results in irreversible brain damage. It would be reasonable to assume that anything which would increase blood flow and oxygenation of the brain will result in better brain cell functioning.

Since our spirit reflects through our brain, anything which would improve brain function would also result in our spirit being uplifted. Certain forms of meditation/exercises (e.g. yoga and aikido) are probably better to vitalize the spirit within us than our traditional Western exercises. More about these later (Chapter 12).

## Conclusion

Physical activity does convince the body of the correct way to go and provides one of the goals leading toward body-mind-spirit unification. A reasonable amount of good physical activity increases the flow of blood to the tissues and actually rejuvenates the cells. It helps flush out from the tissues the waste products of metabolism. It relaxes the body. Exercise not only relaxes the mind, but also increases mental acuity. You begin to think more clearly. Along with this emotions improve and the spirit within comes alive.

## CHAPTER 12

# BENEFITS OF THE
# MEDITATIVE EXERCISES

*John Schumacher and J. Frederick Tresselt*

Most Westerners are still relatively unfamiliar with the benefits which can be derived from some of the physical disciplines that originated in the East. Many have shunned away from either learning or getting involved with some of them (e.g., yoga, Tai Chi) because of a misconception that they are occult or religious practices.

There are other Eastern disciplines, such as karate and judo, which have been less threatening to the Western mind. In fact, interest in these two aggressive self-defense arts have been increasing over the past 20 to 30 years.

In my opinion, several of these Eastern-derived disciplines are ideal for learning body-mind-spirit integration. We have chosen to discuss **yoga** and **aikido**, which are the two we offer and employ at our Center—**yoga** being a more passive but effective exercise one can perform alone or in a group; **aikido** being a **non-aggressive** Martial Art one can practice with another or in a group. Both of these exercises are well suited as disciplines to unify body, mind and spirit and to relieve stress.

I am grateful to John Schumacher for his discussion of Yoga and to J. Frederick Tresselt for Aikido.

## Yoga as a method of dealing with stress

People are fond of saying that stress is one of the products of modern living—the result of a fast-paced, complex, interdependent society. That this is true is undeniable, but to say that stress is a product peculiar to contemporary industrial society is a far cry from the truth. The fact of the matter is that stress is an integral part of life and always has been, from the first cave man listening to the

117

roarings and crashings of beasts in the night, right up to present day parents in the stands of the Little League ball game rooting for their offspring to score the big one. Everyone experiences stress every day of his or her life, so to speak in terms of avoiding stress is misleading and futile. Stress in unavoidable.

Nor is it always negative. Stress can be responsible for motivating the artist to paint a picture, or the engineer to solve a problem. It can create a situation that spurs the individual or group into creative, constructive action. Stress is not only unavoidable, it is sometimes a positive, perhaps even desirable, stimulus.

The question then occurs: when is stress negative, when is it positive?

From what has already been said, one would be led to the supposition that stress that results in constructive action is positive, and stress that produces harmful effects is negative. That sounds reasonable, but there is a problem with defining stress as a function of the results it produces. It implies that it is the stress itself that incurs negative or positive results, and this simply isn't so. What really determines whether stress is negative or positive is the manner in which the individual handles it. What might be a devastating occurrence for one individual might just be the needed stimulus to overcome inertia for another.

The key, therefore, to handling stress lies in the effectiveness of the method of coping with it, which brings me to the topic under discussion: yoga as a method of dealing with stress.

Yoga is a system developed thousands of years ago to enable the individual to consciously expand his awareness of himself, to divine his true inner nature. Although a variety of different schools of yoga exist, all are concerned with the integration of the individual within himself, and then of the unified individual with the cosmos as a whole. In fact the word **yoga** is derived from the Sanskrit word **yuj**, meaning to yoke together or unite, and it is this experience of unity that is the goal of yogic practice.

In describing man's essential nature, the yogic system speaks of him as having three primary aspects, or bodies: the physical, the astral, and the causal. For our purposes we will translate these as the physical, the psychological or mental, and the spiritual. The practice of yoga is designed to bring about the integration and balancing of these physical, mental, and spiritual aspects within the individual. The emphasis on internal integrity and the wide range of techniques and practices that are utilized to bring about that state are what make yoga so effective as a method of dealing with stress. Very few approaches are comprehensive. Indeed the unification and balancing of the three primary aspects of the individual constitute a truly holistic approach to health and growth. This is essential for any real success in dealing with stress, for weakness in any of the three bodies increases vulnerability to the destructive influences of stress, while physical, psychological, and spiritual well-being provide a strong foundation for effectively handling stress.

In considering the practice of yoga any serious approach involves attention to exercise, relaxation, diet, breathing, and meditation. Although we will look at how each of these affects the way a person perceives and handles stress, it is important to bear in mind throughout the discussion that in actual practice, these facets of yoga operate synergistically. Each is important and beneficial in dealing with stress, but as a whole, their combined effects are substantially greater.

Yogic approaches to exercise, relaxation, and diet work directly on the physical body to reduce tension caused by stress. It is important to realize that this tension is a major contributor to stress in and of itself, creating a cycle that feeds itself until interrupted by some method that eliminates the external sources of stress and/or reduces the tension in the body. A body that is in a constant state of tension is inevitably fatigued. Its resistance to illness is lowered, and its ability to withstand further stress is decreased; thus it is vital that physical tension be preceived and controlled.

Yoga exercises, or **asanas,** are an unparalleled way of learning to be aware of tension in the body and to gain control of the body so that tension can be reduced.

The purpose of the **asanas** is to bring one's awareness of the body to a finely tuned state; to regain the ability to perceive the myriads of signals that one's body is contantly sending and which, when properly observed, direct one in the appropriate manner of caring for it; and to free the flow of energy, or **prana,** in the body. It is the blocking of the flow of **prana** that causes tension, and the **asanas** are specifically designed to break up the blocks (which can be caused by any number of things) and allow the **prana** to move freely. As the vital force moves through the various organs, nerves, and muscles of the body, it recharges and cleanses them, making them strong and whole.

The awareness of **prana** and the effects the **asanas** have on its movement are what make **asanas** different from calisthenics or gymnastics. Contrary to popular opinion, control of the body and the remarkable degree of flexibility, strength, and balance that can be attained by the practice of **asanas** are not the result of forcing the body into painful contortions or stretching oneself to the point of agony. Doing so is, in fact, completely contrary to the proper way of practicing **asanas** and is hardly illustrative of subtle tuning or refined awareness. It is, instead, ignorance, deliberate or otherwise, of the body's reasonable limits and is actually counterproductive in terms of physical well-being. The proper way to practice **asanas** is to focus one's awareness of that point just short of real physical discomfort, so that maximum benefits are gained and no harm is done. This is not nearly as easy as it may sound, because the edge between maximum beneficial stretch and/or endurance and pain is a fine one. It requires intense concentration to avoid falling short of or slipping past the edge, not only that, the edge is constantly moving. One is more or less flexible or strong from day to day, even from second to second within the **asana**, so to stay on the edge requires constant awareness. This awareness, which becomes increasingly refined through consistent practice, enables one to readily perceive tension in the body. Many people are completely unaware of the tension in their bodies that stress has created. These people have almost no chance of relieving this tension, because they don't even know it's there. What the **asanas** can do is to make that person aware of the tension, thereby enabling him to do something about it.

One of the things one can do about stress and the tension that results is to relax. Of course everyone would like it to be as easy as simply saying so, but there is more to it than that. Practicing the **asanas** is helpful, because while properly performing them, one learns to use only those parts of the body necessary to do the **asana** and to relax everything else. This ability to differentiate and specify the parts of the body leads to much more efficient use of energy in the body, thereby reducing fatigue and increasing available strength and endurance. This in turn enables one to reduce tension and cope with stress more effectively.

There is also a specific practice of relaxation which is part of any regular yoga practice. After one has performed a series of **asanas**, one relaxes in a reclining **asana** called **shavasana**, or the corpse pose, used especially for relaxation. While in **shavasana** one systematically and consciously relaxes each part of the body, finally focusing the attention on the movement of the breath, maintaining awareness of it as it enters and as it leaves the body. Tests preformed on yoga students during **shavasana** reveal a decrease in heart and respiration rate and a relative decrease in muscular contraction as measured by an electromyograph, a device used to measure the degree of relaxation and contraction of a muscle. Anyone who has practiced the technique of **shavasana** has no doubt about its efficacy for providing a markedly more relaxed state.

After learning the technique of **shavasana** one is able to generalize the relaxed state (although not to the same degree) to situations outside of formal yoga practice by having become familiar with what it feels like to be constantly relaxed. And the practice of

**shavasana** need not be confined to the regular yoga session. Any-time one becomes aware of being under stress and feels tension mounting, doing **shavasana** for five or ten minutes can be just the respite needed to enable one to face the stressful situation with renewed vigor and a more calm demeanor. Of course it isn't always possible to do this, but when it is, the benefits are immediate and definite.

An important point to make at this stage of the discussion is that, although various **asanas** and relaxation techniques can be very helpful in relieving the symptoms of stress, this is not to say that every time one feels stress he should go off and stand on his head or lie down in **shavasana**. These practices are not pills to be taken to relieve unpleasant symptoms, although they may sometimes serve that purpose. They require regular practice to be properly performed. It is this consistent, long-term practice that reveals their primary value as means of providing avenues leading toward a more conscious awareness of the dynamics of one's life and giving one the keen understanding and strength to deal with situations that are creating stress.

The use of diet to reduce tension, increase physical well-being, and foster emotional equilibrium, all important assets in coping with stress, is a more subtle process than the practice of **asanas** and yogic relaxation, but no less effective.

Yogis hold that the types of food one eats have a direct bearing on one's personality. Different kinds of foods fall predominantly into one of three categories. These categories, called **gunas**, de-scribe not only food types, but the properties of all matter. The three **gunas** are the **rajas, tamas,** and **sattva gunas.** The **rajas guna** implies properties associated with activity, movement, force-fulness; the **tamas guna**—inertia, lethargy, inactivity; and **sattva guna**—balance, wholeness, harmony. This is a very simplified and superficial depiction of an extremely complex tenet of yogic phi-losophy, but for our present purposes it will do.

Few, if any, foods fall completely into one category; likewise, few, if any, people can be described as belonging to only one type. It is a question of prevalent tendencies.

According to this system, foods that are stimulating (e.g., spices, coffee, meat, etc.) are said to be **rajasic**, and people who eat **rajasic** foods tend to be **rajasic** in nature, i.e., high-strung, aggres-sive, tense and so on. Impure, overripe, and refined foods are **tamasic** and people who eat them tend towards dullness and lazi-ness. **Sattvic** foods (grains, dairy, fruits, nuts, vegetables) direct one toward better health and psychological equanimity.

This is not to say that one should always shun all **rajasic** and **tamasic** foods or that they are necessarily bad. Nor are all **sattvic** foods necessarily appropriate for every individual. The yogic approach to diet is the same as the approach to **asanas** or relaxation. It involves awareness — awareness of one's own needs, abilities, and limitations. To try to force oneself to adhere to a diet that one reads about in a book may create more stress instead of reducing it. What is needed is careful attention to the effects of certain foods on your own physical and mental state and a willingness to explore and experiment. This is an area where the practice of **asanas** can be very important and where the inter-relatedness of the various yogic practices becomes evident. The fine-tuning and increased ability to read the body's signals that result from the continued practice of **asanas** enable you to see much more clearly what the things you eat are doing to and for you.

As important as attention to what you eat is how and where you eat it. No matter how pure and wholesome the foods you eat, if the dining table is a daily battleground, or if you're grabbing bites while dodging cars on the freeway, the nourishing qualities of your food will be obviated to a large extent. In situations involving conflict or tension, the body's energy, **prana**, is busy contending with the stressful situation and cannot really concern itself with digesting food. Besides which, one has usually not given proper attention to chewing the food, and this adds further to the inevitable indigestion. Under these circumstances even normally beneficial foods can putrefy within the system and produce toxins that weaken the body and make it more vulnerable to stress.

Meals consisting of fresh, properly prepared foods appropriate to one's own needs taken in comfortable congenial surroundings can be a major contribution in the reduction of tension and provide the good health necessary to cope with stress.

Much of what has been said thus far has centered on the physical nature of man, emphasizing the importance of maintaining physical well-being as a bulwark against the onslaughts of stress and illustrating that by working with the body in a conscious, consistent manner, one's mental awareness is sharpened as well.

Two branches of yoga that work in a direct way on one's mental aspect are yogic breathing and meditation.

Breathing exercises, or **pranayama,** are perhaps the most fundamental of all yogic techniques. We have talked about **prana** as energy, or vital force. The word **yama** means control, so **pranayama** is the control of energy. Breath is equated with this vital force; thus one gains control of the **prana** in one's body by practicing specific breathing exercises, either by themselves or in connection with the **asanas.**

Of course breath is part of everything one does, whether is be exercising, thinking, relaxing, or just sitting. All this seems obvious, but how aware of your breathing are you? Even superficial attention to breathing reveals that it affects and reflects both the physical and the mental.

For example, let's say a person becomes angry. What happens? His breath becomes short, erratic. Usually his body tightens up, his fists and jaws clench, and his face may redden. Now suppose he were to take ten deep breaths. Almost invariably the anger decreases, and the body becomes less tense. When the breath was short and erratic, it **reflected** the man's physical and emotional state. Subsequently, the deep breaths **affected** his physical and emotional state.

As another example, let's try a little experiment. Stop reading right now and listen very carefully for the next ten seconds to the sounds occurring right near you, whatever they are. Listen hard . . . What happened to your breathing? It probably stopped, didn't it? What happened to the usual parade of thoughts that marches through your mind. They stopped, too, didn't they? When your thought processes stopped briefly so that you could listen, your breathing stopped as well.

The purpose of all this is to illustrate how intrinsically the breath is related to both the physical and mental aspects of the individual. It is obviously physical, and it also has an undeniable relationship to one's mental state, which is why **pranayama** is so valuable as a means of working with stress. The mind and the emotions are subtle and elusive. It is not easy to work with them. For some people it's practically impossible. But nearly everyone can work with the body to some degree. When one begins studying and practicing **pranayama,** one begins with a basic physical function. It is not necessarily easy, but it is definitely possible for the majority of people to practice some form of **pranayama.** And while one is working on the physical level with **pranayama,** one is affecting the mental nature as well. With consistent practice the bridge that the breath provides between the mental and the physical becomes more apparent, and as it does, the elusive mental states become more accessible. One becomes aware of the way that breathing is affected by the mind, and conversely, one begins to see that breathing can in turn affect mental and emotional states. Control of the breath leads to control of the mind, and as a result of this control, one develops the poise and equanimity to deal with stressful situations.

That the use of breathing exercises can produce such effects should not be surprising. Natural childbirth classes, for example, have utilized breathing techniques with very positive results, and labor and giving birth can certainly be stressful.

While **pranayama** is the bridge between the physical and the mental, broadening the path that inherently exists between the two, the practice of meditation lies in the realm of the mind.

A wide variety of meditation techniques exists, but they all have the common goal of leading the meditator to an understanding of his own inner nature and from that point, to an understanding of the nature of the universe. This in fact is the ultimate goal of yoga and is the purpose of the various practices.

To understand one's inner nature, it is necessary that the mind be still. Whatever method one employs to achieve this, in the process one must confront the contents of the mind, for they will surely display themselves as the meditator seeks stillness.

The process of observing the mind, of seeing the thoughts and feelings that arise, is valuable in terms of providing a psychological framework for dealing with stress. For one thing, the objectivity fostered by the practice of meditation creates a space between the individual and the source of stress. Stress usually presents itself as mental and emotional pressure, and often one is so wrapped up in the anxieties and tensions associated with the stressful situation that clear perception of the situation is practically impossible. One winds up fumbling about in the darkness and confusion of the pressurized environment, unable to distinguish himself from his circumstances. Meditation gives him the chance to make that distinction, and once he no longer identifies himself with the stressful situation, much of the energy that was being drained into anxiety and tension can be used to handle the source of stress.

Another result of the objectivity stimulated by meditation is an increased awareness of responsibility. The individual begins to see that, in many instances, the things that seemed to be happening to him purely by chance are, in reality, closely related to attitudes he has maintained and actions he has performed. One begins to see that he plays the dominant role in shaping the world around him, and that whether or not he succumbs to or overcomes the pressures placed on him is largely in his hands.

This is only one of the ways that practicing meditation gradually gives one a different perspective on life. Some things that once seemed very important lose their sense of urgency; often there is growing desire to simplify one's life as one sees how unnecessarily complex things have become. The simpler and more straightforward one's life, the easier it is to manage it, thereby decreasing the occurrence of stress.

It is important to point out that things like simplification and objectification mentioned above are not goals or conditions placed on the meditator, but tend instead to occur as a result of meditation. One of the things many people are inclined to do is place a number of internal and external demands on themselves. By their nature, demands are either fulfilled or unfulfilled, which is to say one is either successful or unsuccessful with regard to fulfilling them. The fear of failure is a common source of stress. It creates pressure on the individual.

The way that meditation works in helping to reduce the stress associated with feelings of failure and inadequacy is to promote the quality of acceptance. When one meditates, thoughts and insights that are not always to one's liking inevitably appear. The usual reaction is to push them away, to hide from them; but one sees that the very act of suppression is itself disquieting to the mind. Not only that, the same thoughts invariably arise again. The way to free the mind from these thoughts is to dispassionately observe them, to accept them as a part of oneself. Only through their acceptance does one have the opportunity to move beyond them to stillness. Meditation leads one toward seeing oneself as he really is, and learning to accept that reality is a powerful tool for reducing stress.

So far the discussion has centered on some of the ways that different yoga practices can help one to cope with stress by considering their effects primarily on the physical and mental bodies of the individual. Little has been said of the spiritual nature, which, according to yogic teaching, is the true inner nature of man.

When meditation was first mentioned, it was said that the goal of yoga was to understand one's inner nature, from that to understand the nature of the universe. For this to happen, the mind must be still, for until the mind is still, all the meditator can hope to understand is the workings of the mind, and although this can be of inestimable value, particularly as it relates to stress management, still it falls short of the goal. The reason is that the mind does not truly reflect the inner nature of man nor does his body. His inner nature is revealed in his spiritual body — that part of him through which he experiences ultimate interconnectedness with the universe around him. Through the practice of yoga, one gradually becomes aware of the underlying unity beneath the apparent diversity that surrounds him. He begins to understand that he is an inseparable part of the whole process of existence, that there is a fundamental essence within him that is conjoined with that unified whole. That essence is his spiritual body. And as his awareness of first the existence and then the nature of his spiritual self grows, an inevitable balance and calmness manifest themselves in his being. It is this equanimity and the strengthened propensity to seek the truth that provide the best tools of all for perceiving and handling stress, because from this vantage point, stressful situations are simply opportunities to discover deeper, more subtle aspects of one's true nature. One welcomes them as means to strip away the false and useless and get to the core of things.

Thus as a result of the process of increasingly refined awareness of the three aspects of his being brought about by continuous, conscientious practice of the various yogic techniques, the individual becomes integrated, strong, whole, and thereby capable of dealing with the obstacles and opportunities he encounters in his life. He becomes aware of the way stress is affecting his body and mind, and he develops the clarity to see what the situations are that create that stress.

## Aikido and stress

Aikido is a new Japanese Martial Art which was discovered by the West in the 1940's. Its founder, Morihei Ueshiba, developed Aikido according to the "laws of nature." He taught that the ultimate expression of Aikido is love. Today Aikido is practiced by thousands of students throughout the world. There are probably as many reasons for the study of Aikido as there are students, but there is one modern-day challenge that concerns us all.

More and more people today are becoming conscious of the need to reduce stress. Today's fast-paced existence, pressures in the job market, and inflation, all create the probability of stress. Stress usually results in an excessive wear and tear on the body, mind, and spirit. How can Aikido help us reduce the amount of stress in our lives? To answer this question we shall explore three aspects of Aikido: the physical, mental and spiritual.

When a student begins the study of Aikido the foremost goal is to get the body in shape. Good physical condition is a prerequisite to the study of Aikido arts. Moreover, it is essential to continued good health. Before any practice of the actual arts there is a period of exercise. The exercises consist of stretching all the muscles, ligaments, tendons and joints in positions that coincide with the natural movement of the body. Many of these stretching exercises are similar to Hatha Yoga. The result of these exercises is a relaxed and conditioned body.

Following these exercises we then enter into specific Aikido training. In his book *This is Aikido,* Koichi Tohei explains that there are four basic concepts to apply before practice: *relaxation, extension of Ki, centering and weight underside.*

*Ki* is defined as *inner energy* or *spiritual energy.* A few examples may illustrate *Ki* better than a wordy explanation. A Karate student uses *Ki* when he concentrates his energy on one point for the purpose of breaking boards. In Aikido this same energy is more free-flowing and is used to keep the body strong and relaxed. *Ki* is also evident in extreme circumstances. We have all heard stories about someone lifting a car off an injured person or an athlete who has performed beyond himself in a sport. *Ki* is the ever present energy of the universe. In Aikido one learns to tap this universal energy. *Centering* is important in achieving relaxation of the body. This center of "one point" is where *Ki* flows to and from. *Centering* is not only important in the practice of Aikido, it is also useful in our daily experiences. Tensing the body uses unnecessay energy. *Centering* keeps our body relaxed and prepared to respond to any situation.

*Weight underside* is maintained through the posture to achieve total relaxation. When sitting down or standing straight, it is easy to be relaxed, but as we move it becomes more difficult. For example, our arm can lift our whole upper body and change your center of balance, but keeping the weight of our arm on the bottom side makes it much easier to maintain a calm position.

All of these aids to relaxation help to reduce stress in a physical sense. Having a rested and calm body is an important step in achieving a healthy attitude.

To create less stress at the mental level we must first learn to relax the mind. In Aikido there are many forms of breathing exercises. Respiration is the one function that links the body and mind. The major method of breathing in Aikido is called *Misogi*. *Misogi* is a purification exercise starting with deep inhalation through the nose. The air settles in the abdomen instead of the chest. When the air is settled and the body relaxed, there is complete exhalation through the mouth. This practice is done with the eyes half open for twenty to thirty minutes. The results of this breathing are very similar to meditation. It is in a sense a breathing meditation. With the use of these physical and mental relaxation techniques we can now explore how to maintain this calm state.

*Ki* has been described as an **inner** or **spiritual energy.** Physically we feel this energy in our practice of Aikido techniques. The mental aspect of *Ki* is control. Combining all the ideas of harmony, prefection and flowing, it is evident that there is a need for control. Imagine an Aikidoist with tremendous energy performing a self-defense art with no control on a beginning student.

Aikido training also teaches us how to be receptive. Being receptive is learning from as well as teaching fellow students. There is a story in Japan about a man who thought he was very wise. His tea cup was always filled. So when he went from house to house in the village he could not accept any more tea. Another wise man always kept his tea cup empty. He could always accept tea, then decide to drink it or throw it away. The story illustrates the idea of receptiveness. We can all learn from each other if we allow ourselves to have an empty cup. This also relates to the philosophy of no competition. It is less stressful and more fun to learn and share ideas than to think you always have the correct answers.

The world most of us experience is highly competitive. Competition for jobs, social positions, sports, and even personal affections create fast paced stressful conditions. In determining how to deal with these challenges we must be aware of their existence. In Aikido the philosophy of nonresistance does not mean we allow the world to trample over us. It means moving with the forces, not becoming caught up in them.

Aikido is practiced intensely. We strive to develop perfection of the arts in our everyday lives. Intense activity is always beneficial to good health and the reduction of stress because our minds need a place to be at peace. It is the place where we can filter and refine all our thoughts. Ultimately, life events are viewed in proper perspective.

The study of *Ki* starts on the physical level, then we learn to lead and control it on the mental level. Eventually, it becomes a natural part of us. We all have *Ki*, it is everywhere. Through the study of Aikido **we become aware of it within ourselves.** Through this awareness we learn our connection with the whole universe. Spirituality represents the culmination of the development, awareness, and harmony a person achieves within and without. As one develops spiritually, whether it be through Aikido or any other discipline, stress diminishes. Ultimately there is no stress because there is no conflict, no competition, and no differences. Man and nature are one. The founder and great master of Aikido, Morhei Ueshiba, always said, "Aikido is practiced for the love and protection of all things."

# CHAPTER 13

# STRESS RELATED TO PHYSICAL HEALTH

## Physical dis-ease interferes with coping ability

Physical illness puts a strain on your ability to cope with challenging situations. Physical dis-ease consumes our energy, and this loss of energy affects our reserve capacity to respond to other situations tapping our systems.

Visualize for a moment a water tank within your home. The pumping system has been set to maintain a pressure of 60 pounds per square inch (p.s.i.). Consider that when the water flows through the pipes, the resistance within those pipes is negligible, and when you open a single faucet the water will flow out at a force equal to the force within the tank, that is 60 pounds p.s.i. What will happen when you open a second faucet? The flow from each faucet will be 30 p.s.i. How about opening a third faucet? The flow will be further reduced to 20 pounds p.s.i. for each faucet. How about opening a fourth and a fifth faucet? As you open more faucets, the force of the water coming out of any single faucet will diminish because the source of the pressure is not increasing to meet the extra needs resulting from opening so many faucets.

Our physical body has a limited source of energy. You can do a lot to improve the efficiency of your machine by being aware of the food you eat, how much you rest the body, etc. However, there is a limitation to what the body can provide.

Dis-ease is like a faucet that remains open all the time. It takes energy just to maintain the body at **status quo.** And it takes energy to repair tissues. If any of you have ever undergone surgery, you will appreciate how such an insult drains the body of energy and how much more food you have to eat just to overcome the shock of surgery. During such times the body goes into what is called a "negative nitrogen balance", and more caloric energy must be provided to return to a positive balance.

You have all known individuals with long standing chronic disease and observed what happens to their capacity to perform. It isn't long before their mind and emotions become affected. You will undoubtly begin to see that their spirit begins to die. They get depressed. They begin to lose their will-to-live.

When you have had a simple cold, your whole body is affected. Simple chores become laborious. Your thinking becomes fuzzy. Not only is your head stopped up, but your mind can't function. Your temper gets short, your emotions labile and your spirit weak. All of this from a simple head cold that you recover from in just a few days.

Be aware of the importance of maintaining a state of physical wellness. Keep your reserves up so that you can handle life's challenges in a positive manner for your upward evolvement.

## Physical dis-ease causing and resulting from stress

It would take many volumes to discuss the stress-related illnesses. As with many physical dis-eases, an illness may be either the cause or result of stress, or both. As discussed earlier, any disease state can interfere with your ability to cope with what would otherwise be a normal life event. In this section, I would like to mention a number of stress-related physical dis-eases common in our culture today, and discuss only a few of them.

Table 12-1 lists some of the stress-related illnesses common to our present day culture. The list is by no means all-inclusive. It is worth discussing a few of these to examine how stress is involved and how you might approach their treatment with total balance, that is, holistically.

**Pain.** Acute and chronic pain can probably be considered as two separate and distinct entities. Although they may be related, since acute pain can go on to develop into chronic pain, the body seems to deal with these two entities differently.

Generally, the degree of pain is related to three events; the actual physical pain coming from tissue destruction, one's memory of previous pain, and one's emotional reaction to the pain. Most authorities agree that the later two events contribute much more to an individual's pain experience than the former. This is especially true for chronic pain. Any treatment modality which does not consider these factors usually does not result in significant pain relief.

Acute pain is usually the result of tissue damage (e.g. a bruise, cut in skin, broken arm or leg, ulcers, head injury, etc.) or of altered physiology which stimulates the acute pain fibers throughout the body (e.g., acute headaches, colic, possibly muscle spasm, etc.)

**Table 12-1**
**Some Stress-Related Physical Illnesses**
**Common to our Culture**

**Pain:**
  acute and chronic
**Headache:**
  tension, migraine, cluster-migraine
**Cardiovascular dis-ease:**
  high blood pressure
  angina pectoris
  coronary heart dis-ease
**Asthma**
**Gastrointestinal dis-ease:**
  stomach & duodenal ulcers
  colitis
  spastic colon
  Crohn's dis-ease
  constipation
**Arthritis:**
  degenerative and rheumatoid
**Collagen dis-eases:**
  lupus erythematosis
  periarteritis nodosum
  rheumatoid arthritis
**Auto-immune dis-ease:**
  collagen dis-ease
  multiple sclerosis
**Allergy**
**Obesity**
**Cancer**

This form of pain usually subsides after the tissues have repaired themselves or the altered physiological changes have normalized.

Chronic pain appears to have several causative factors among which actual tissue destruction probably contributes the least. Other factors, usually psychological, result in a pain image which can alter the body's ability to control the pain. Somehow, the body's intrinsic *endorphin* system doesn't function properly. The administration of pain killers to control chronic pain usually further suppresses the body's pain controlling mechanisms. As a result increased dosage and stronger pain medications are prescribed, further aggravating the situation.

An individual experiencing chronic pain eventually loses faith in his ability to control his dis-ease and eventually he may become discouraged and depressed. His ability to cope with otherwise normal life situations is seriously compromised. At this point, the pain worsens and there develops a self-perpetuating illness state.

Successful therapy lies in the individual's firm desire to eliminate his chronic pain by developing a new and positive attitude toward his condition. He must reactivate intrinsic pain controlling centers. Such is the approach of C. Norman Shealy, M.D. and his group at the Pain and Health Rehabilitation Center in LaCrosse, Wisconsin. They successfully employ biofeedback and other treatment modalities with chronic pain patients who have not been helped by conventional treatments.

Even if you are one of those individuals who feels hopelessly plagued by chronic pain, you have the ability to change your attitude if you want to, and in so doing open up new avenues to handle an old situation. "As a man thinketh in his heart (and mind), so is he."

**Headache.** Headaches can be acute and chronic. Both forms can not only be the result of such factors as improper diet, allergies, tension, etc., but also cause further tension and upheaval hampering your ability to cope. Anyone who has experienced a headache knows how difficult it is to control his emotions and to use his mind constructively. Migraine and cluster migraine headaches are particularly disturbing because they are usually more severe, longer in duration, and chronic in nature.

The drug companies would like you to think that they have the pills to help you handle your headache. We now know that depending on medications can actually prevent you from solving your basic challenge. There are many ways one can treat headaches. However, unless the basic cause is determined and handled or treated, the symptoms may come and go.

I will relate a personal story because of its relevance to the treatment of migraine headaches and my introduction to the holistic approach in my profession.

In January, 1976, I started to experience what eventually was diagnosed as cluster migraine headaches. I had them on three previous occasions during the months of December and January of 1967, '68, and '69. There was a family history of cluster migraines — my mother for many years experienced them. She had been diagnosed as being highly allergic to rabbits and she was constantly knitting angora sweaters. The source of her allergy was eliminated and eventually she was cured.

In my case I was undergoing tremendous personal challenges in my private life. It had already been determined that I was allergic to almost every animal that had fur. I was living on a farm but had not been experiencing symptoms for 5 years. I sought the advice of physicians, eventually a neurologist, who sympathized and prescribed ergotamine. The headaches were relentless. I increased the dosage of ergotamine to 4 to 5 times the upper tolerant level just to keep the headaches to a point where I could function. I always had a headache and, if lucky, I would get 2 to 3 hours sleep each night. On three separate days I was unable to work at all. I could not remember having missed a day of work because of sickness. All kinds of tests were performed. I had an abnormal EEG; additional tests were ordered. At this point I threw up my hands and said that I had had enough. I felt my whole life falling apart. I was becoming depressed.

My sister, a nurse living in San Diego, asked me to come out to take a "mind science" course to cure myself of the headaches. I was reluctant to do so. My mind was closed to new ideas. Eventually, I decided to go for I had nothing to lose. The headaches were getting worse and I couldn't visualize any improvement. Everything else had failed.

To make a long story short, I went out to San Diego and took the course. On the third day of what could best be described as a meditation/mind awareness course, I was able to rid myself of the headaches, and I have never had another headache since. In fact, I am no longer susceptible to that malady.

I immediately recognized the value of such an approach and wondered why conventional medicine did not use this modality. I began to explore the possibilities of sharing my experience with others and have since devoted much time and effort toward establishing an holistic facility devoted to achieving a new perspective on life and health. The philosophy of the Center is to combine the knowledge of modern medical science with the newly developing awareness of alternative healing methods.

It is most interesting to observe the reactions of others upon my return from having taken the meditation/mind science course and having been free of the cluster migraine headaches.

My friends were happy and were convinced that I had experienced a miracle. The reaction of many others who knew me less ranged from "well, that's very interesting, his headaches were in his mind to begin with!" to individuals who were convinced that I was somewhere out there in the kooky fringe or that I was involved with evil things bordering on devil-worship.

I had become aware that we do have within ourself the ability and capability of not only creating our own illnesses but also, more importantly, to curing ourselves of the sicknesses we develop. Using this approach is by no means unique as there are many physicians and other individuals in the healing profession who have come to realize the importance of "wholeness" and are now working to deliver this *New Medicine* to the people.

If you experience chronic headaches, seek out the advice of a physician who is aware of the holistic approach. Make sure you don't have any serious life threatening condition accounting for your headaches. Begin to believe in yourself. Mobilize your inner healing powers. Increase your awareness and start living the abundant life.

**Asthma.** Although very seldom is asthma a life-threatening disease, it can cause many apprehensive and frustrating hours. Children may not know that their asthma will not kill them, but you couldn't convince them during an attack when they are literally starved of life giving breath.

As with many dis-ease states which are given names because of the symptoms they produce, asthma has many causes. Make serious attempts to discover the causes of an individual's asthma, whether it be due to an infectious upper respiratory disease, allergy to respiratory inhalents or to foods, etc. A treatment program then can be devised to eliminate the underlying causative factors.

As with most of the dis-eases listed in Table 12-1, there are psychological factors contributing to the asthma experience. I do believe that asthma can be controlled and cured by the power we have within us even when the disease is known to be due to specific allergens.

I am reminded of a story a mother told me about her son who had his first asthma attack at the age of 7 years. On the initial visit to the doctor for that illness, the boy heard the doctor tell the mother that eventually the child would grow out of his asthma and probably would not have another attack after his 14th birthday. The boy's asthma progressed over the next several years and all the boy would say was he couldn't wait till his 14th birthday when he would never have asthma again. Up until the day before that birthday he had several attacks. On his 14th birthday he rejoiced. When the mother was telling me the story her son was 18 years old. He never had an attack of asthma after his 14th birthday! Now, I ask you, what was so different about his *external* environment after his birthday that would have influenced his dis-ease so dramatically? Absolutely nothing.

But, what happened to his *internal* environment on his 14th birthday? Plenty. On that day he put into motion the power behind his *belief factor,* probably *the most powerful force for healing* we have within ourselves. Let us also consider that this same boy at the age of seven allowed (subconsciously) the words and belief of his doctor to influence his condition with the prediction that the child would experience asthma during the period from age 7 to 14 years. Thank God, the physician gave him an escape which was that on his 14th birthday he would be free of asthma.

We mentioned before, and will go into more detail later, that *faith* and *belief* is a double edged sword. It is the same faith that dooms you to a dis-ease as cures you. The only difference is the emphasis, the polarity you give it.

I had asthma for 7 years, three of those years while working at the National Institute of Health. Not a day went by when I didn't have three full blown asthma attacks (and I never lost a day's work.) When I got rid of my headaches in 1976, I cured myself of asthma also. I have never had an attack since. As with the headaches, I am not susceptible to asthma anymore! Furthermore, I take every opportunity to frequently affirm: "I am not susceptible to headaches or asthma." This type of reinforcement does repeatedly remind the subconscious mind to eventually demonstrate the truth of this automatically (Chapter 17).

**Auto-immune dis-ease.** Many readers may not be aware of a group of illnesses, referred to as *auto-immune dis-eases.* The essential feature of these dis-ease states is that the body for some unknown reason develops antibodies against its own tissues. Antibodies are substances made within our body to destroy foreign substances, such as dis-ease-producing bacteria, viruses and parasites. It is not good to develop antibodies which would destroy your own kidney (certain forms of nephritis), joints (rheumatoid arthritis), heart (rheumatic fever), nerves (most likely multiple sclerosis), small arteries (periarteritis nodosum), etc.

This situation is probably opposite to that existing in the cancer patient whose immune surveillance system, which should detect and destroy abnormal cells, is not functioning. With auto-immune dis-ease there is a mis-programming and the immune system believes some of the tissues are foreign and sets out to destroy them.

I believe that these systems can be controlled by centers under the direction of the central communication center, our brain. Further research is needed to prove this point. However, in the meantime there is good reason to operate under this assumption.

Any person experiencing an auto-immune dis-ease appreciates the chronic nature of his condition. If he gets depressed and loses additional energy, his dis-ease progresses. His coping ability is compromised. We offer hope to these individuals, but we are quick to modify this hope by saying that *successful self-cure is but an attitude or belief factor away.*

**Cancer.** Probably the most dreaded dis-ease facing our society today is cancer. It is often synonymous with death. You must, of course, change this belief within the subconscious of the cancer patient before he can begin to effect a cure.

As mentioned above, with cancer the basic defect probably lies in the immune surveillance system, a system which should recognize, detect and destroy abnormal cancer cells originating with the body. The average individual produces tens of thousands of abnormal, potentially cancerous, cells daily. The immune surveillance system does its job to clean these cells out of the body. In the cancer patient this system is not functioning properly. However, I believe, as many others do also, that an individual can reactivate this system to perform as it is intended. Readers are referred to the work of O. Carl Simonton, M.D., C. Norman Shealy, M.D. (The Pain and Health Rehabilitation Center, La Crosse, Wisconsin) and Nicola M. Tauraso, M.D. (The GOTACH Center for Health, Frederick, MD) for further information about work being performed along these lines.

## General considerations

As mentioned earlier, the purpose of this chapter is not to discuss in detail all dis-ease states causing and resulting from stress, but rather to describe several more common dis-ease states to acquaint you with the mechanisms involved. Simply stated, all physical dis-eases result in drainage of energy, the same energy that the individual needs to employ in coping. Any condition causing an energy drain seriously interferes with your ability to "keep your head above the water," as the saying goes. But, our aim should be more than just to keep our head above the water.

Any drainage of energy causes the physical dis-eases to deteriorate further, thus making the unwanted negative situation self-perpetuating.

Begin looking at your physical dis-eases as manifestations of your not taking full responsibility and control. Begin to examine the psychodynamics, the reasons why you think and act as you do and why you experience the dis-eases you do. Execute a program of self-health. Regenerate your intrinsic energy stores and begin to experience the fullness of life maintaining that fantastic state of physical, mental, emotional, and spiritual wellness, which is our destiny.

# CHAPTER 14

# STRESS RELATED TO MENTAL AND EMOTIONAL HEALTH

## Mental attitude affecting coping ability

*The mind is where it's at!* What separates us from all other forms of life here on earth? It is our mind (and, of course, our very special spirit or soul). Man has the capacity to think. Man also has a free will, so he can choose either to think constructively or destructively. His choice will determine how he lives and what he is going to get out of life. It is at the mind dimension that man uses his imagination, one of the three keys to mind awareness. It is most important that we use our imagination constructively to create the positive conditions we want to experience in life (Chapter 7). Since we are creative beings, we can begin to exercise this creativity at the mind dimension on a **conscious** level.

We have all heard the expression, "It's all in his mind." How often do we hear ourselves admit that a particular situation is all in **my** mind? We are more ready to observe and judge that our fellow man has a particular challenge in his mind, than we are to admit that we too are responsible for thoughts we create.

There is a reason why we say "it is in his mind." It is because we subconsciously acknowledge the importance of our thoughts. The challenge appears when we translate this belief to our conscious mind and outwardly acknowledge this fact.

When we acknowledge that we and no one else are responsible for our thoughts, our actions and deeds, and even our state of wellness or our state of dis-ease, we can begin to look forward to a whole new outlook toward life.

It is an all too human error to blame someone else. "He made me do it. She made me do it." How about when in jest we say: "The devil made me do it!" Be careful. Please, **do not** jest when you're dealing with the mind dimension. When you think of something you make a mental picture, and it is this mental picture that gets recorded permanently onto your brain cells. When you verbalize the thought, you add energy to it and the impression on your brain cells become greater. The subsciousnes mind does not know the negative; it acts in a literal way. It recognizes only the picture. When you say that you do not want to think about an orange, you have already created the picture of the very thing you did not want. Once the picture is created, it is too late to negate it. However, once we are aware of this action, it can be replaced by a picture of your choice. Remember the game: "I want you to think about everything but a banana. Empty your mind if you have to, but do not think of a banana." You know what happens! The only thing you can think about is that banana.

The same is true when you create negative pictures even if they were in jest. Do not subject your mind to *negative creative imaginings.* Carefully scrutinize the words you use (Chapter 7). Carefully scrutinize the movies you watch, especially if you are already troubled with uptight and nervous emotions.

Most importantly, carefully scrutinize what your children watch on TV and the movies. Their imaginations are highly impressionable and their bio-computer brains are absorbing everything.

You should realize the irreparable harm caused by exposing children's minds to scare and fear. Through ignorance of the power of the subconscious, we allow our children's mind to be influenced — by negative creative imaginings. We do it every year at Halloween, for instance. These scary images enter the mind at a very receptive young age, and later, years later, rear their ugly heads as increased nervousness, emotional lability, insecurity, and an inability to cope with stressful situations. When it does surface as these other manifestations, we don't understand it. This is because we are not consciously aware of what's going on within the deeper, more hidden recesses of our subconscious mind.

Many of you may feel afraid now because of fears placed into your mind as a child. Don't waste any more energy worrying about it. From now on, you are going to be concerned only about what you are going to create in your mind from this day forward. It is a mistake to rehash the past. When you do, you conjure up these negative pictures and begin to recycle the past. This further reinforces these negative images — the very images you wish to replace.

Active mediation exercises can help you tap your inner mind to give you the mental energy to impress upon your subconscious the results of your positive imaginings. Additionally, it is by employing meditative procedures that you will be able to create the mental visual pictures (that is, you activate, develop, improve, and execute your powers of visualization) needed to further impress upon your subconscious mind the changes you wish to make. Finally, you begin to develop and maintain a positive belief system that you can use your faith constructively rather than destructively against you.

## Emotional instability causing and resulting from stress

Your emotional well-being is, of course, related to the states of your physical and mental health. It is impossible to look at emotions as being an entity having a separate, distinct, and unrelated existence. As an exercise, however, let us look at emotions as a separate part of you and determine how your other parts might be affected by it.

Let us for a moment assume that you are healthy physically and that you are a positive thinker, or as positive as you think you can be, but, that your emotions are unstable. That is, you get upset very easily, you fall apart if a stranger comes into the room, you may cry for no obvious reason. You may anger very easily. You fight a lot. One drink and you punch your best buddy in the nose. You may be downright hostile. You're suspicious of everyone around you. You fear your own shadow. Essentially, you have little or no control of your emotions.

Eventually, you begin to experience physical challenges. You may develop headaches, ulcers, a chronic pain condition, high blood pressure, etc. You begin to experience chronic tiredness. You develop joint pain. Your back aches.

Your appetite begins to be affected: you either lose your appetite or you begin to eat too much. You're somewhat depressed, and, as usually is the case, you decrease your physical activity. You begin to gain weight and get obese, or you lose weight and become too skinny and lose your energy stores. You may begin drinking heavily such items as alcoholic beverages and stimulating drinks such as coffee. You start taking other drugs, tranquilizers, pep pills, sleeping pills, etc. You then start combining alcohol with these "cop out" pills.

Do you see what is happening? All of these other actions further aggravate your frayed emotions. Your obesity may further destroy your self-image. You become dependent and addicted to your "cop out" pills. You get depressed and you begin to wonder whether things will ever improve.

And finally, your spirit begins to die. For many the will-to-live goes down the drain. Within a short period of time you develop a life-threatening dis-ease such as cancer because your subconscious biocomputer mind pushed the self-destruct button.

What may have started as simple emotional instability is now becoming a challenge of great proportion. We have known for a long time of the relationship between emotions and the other states of man. The field of psychosomatic medicine has been concerned with this for years.

I am going through this rather graphic illustration in order that you might consciously appreciate what most of you have already known for years. With your conscious realization of this relationship, you can institute a program of living designed to develop within you a strong emotional character.

The opposite side of the coin should not be ignored. We've all known individuals with strong emotional make-ups. Provided other aspects of their personality are well, their strong solid emotions make a fantastic contribution to their overall state of wellness.

## Mental dis-ease states caused by stress

Table 13-1 lists some of the mental dis-ease states caused by and aggravating stress in man. Many of these have already been discussed in Chapter 5. The main point to make at this time is that these states may not only be caused by stress but they may in themselves be the reason why you have difficulty in adequately handling the vicissitudes of life.

### Table 13-1
### Mental Dis-ease States Caused by
### and Aggravating Stress in Man

Depression and despair
Obsession
Nervous Tension
Chronic Tiredness
Insomnia
Paranoia
Emotional Instability: anger, hatred, fear, anxiety, crying spells, etc.

We are not hermits. We are social beings by nature. Since the dawn of time man has had to interact with his fellow beings. We are part of families which are parts of communities which are parts of larger social structures. There is the world of mankind. Although at times we would like to blame the world for the bad things that happen to us, we must realize that the world represents the collective consciousness of each and every individual. If we wish to change the world, we must start to make changes within ourselves. Taking responsibility for our mental and emotional states is like taking the first step in a long journey. We have the power to make the changes we wish to make within ourselves. We must develop the attitude that what appears to be negative influences around us do not have to affect us and that we can become a positive motivating force for ourselves, families, the community and the world.

Our ability to overcome stress is related to the attitude and energy we maintain. The mental dis-ease states listed in Table 13-1 are high energy draining situations. Experiencing them seriously interferes with our ability to cope. Chapters 15 and 16 describe some of the techniques you can employ to develop the mental and emotional well being needed to be in control of life situations.

Suffice it to say, mental and emotional illnesses result from our inability to cope. **Physical dis-ease is only a mental attitude away.** Just be aware that total health is an interrelationship of body, mind, emotions and spirit. Our approach to total holistic well-being should be multifacted. However, remember that *the mind is where it's at.* Conserve your mental energy and use it wisely.

One of the things lacking in our society is a program to develop and conserve mental energy. For example elementary and secondary schools accent physical education and teach development of the mind in a way which dissipates mental energy. They do not have active programs such as controlled relaxation, meditation, visualization which are designed to develop the reserve electrochemical energy existing within the brain cells of each of us. The lack of such programs show that many are unaware that we really don't have to look elsewhere for our riches.

Russell H. Conwell used to say it eloquently in his talks which were eventually published in the book, *Acres of Diamonds.* I found this book both interesting and enlightening. More individuals are becoming aware of the true strength we have within ourselves. Many have experiences that were once thought to be miracles but are now being considered part of our nature. These are exciting times and you should be happy to be alive here and now.

# CHAPTER 15

# SPIRITUAL HEALTH AND STRESS

## Spiritual laws

Whenever one considers man's spiritual nature, it is essential to recognize that there are spiritual laws that exist and function just as surely and as effectively as physical laws. Although a spiritual law may not always be as apparent nor operate as quickly as a particular physical law, human history clearly shows that spiritual laws cannot be ignored if integration and wholeness are to be achieved.

A necessary step in the understanding of and the coping with stress is learning what the basic spiritual laws are. Throughout the ages these laws have been articulated in many ways by religions. The Noble Eightfold Path of Buddhism, the Ten Commandments of Judaism, and the Sermon on the Mount of Christianity are examples of some of these spiritual laws. The two great commandments that Jesus spoke of, loving God with heart, mind, soul and strength, and loving your neighbor as yourself, are a concise and excellent summary of the spiritual laws.

When you learn these laws and begin to assimilate and integrate them into your daily life, then you are well on the way toward wholeness, not only of spirit, but also of body and mind.

## Spirit as source of health or illness

There are some persons who believe that **all** illness begins in the spirit. Although it is difficult to prove this scientifically, such a belief does raise important questions about the genesis of many illnesses. The spirit (or soul) is the initial principle of being and, if the spirit is weak or wayward, the other aspects of selfhood — body and mind — will suffer accordingly. The New Testament gospels mention several healings by Jesus in which he first healed the spirit, through his forgiving love before he healed the body. These particular healings imply that until the spirit is made whole the body cannot be healed.

To say that all of our physical, mental or emotional ills are due to our wayward or sinful spirits may be extreme. However, there is no question that the health of spirit is inseparably related to the health of your body and mind. This truth needs to be emphasized for too often we seek to solve our stresses and distresses without any reference to or consideration of spirit.

## Some obstacles to a healthy spirit

Obstacles to spiritual health are legion. The following are particularly important.

- **Lust.** This uncontrolled hyperactivity and use of the body's sexual energy brings pleasure for awhile but soon becomes an empty and futile exercise because the mind and spirit are not nurtured. Through lust one of our most precious gifts is abused, and frustration, enslavement, and violence abound.

- **Greed.** Many believe that the excessive accumulation of power, things, and money brings joy, fulfillment and freedom from distress. Actually, the opposite is true. In the greedy person there develops an obsession for possession, a chain reaction of more — ever more. Life becomes unbalanced, proper priorities are prostituted, fear of loss or fear of failure sets in — all of which lead to new and destructive stress situations.

- **Envy and jealousy.** These are negative attitudes that bring isolation and frustration. They are a poison that destroys reason.

- **Anger and the related emotions of resentment, hatred, rage terror.** These energies, deemed to be destructive and sinful by all religious systems, torture the body, torment the mind, and, like the whirlpool, suck the spirit into the depths — the depths of darkness, depression and despair.

- **Fear and anxiety.** These emotions, usually preoccupied with unreality by not dealing with the present moment, are major causes of bodily and mental illness. So often fears feed on pessimism and forget or fail to recognize the power of faith, hope and love.

- **Regret.** Regretful living is fretful living. It is living sadly and remorsefully in the negative aspects of our past. Regret comes from the same root word as grieve, so that to live regretfully is to live tearfully, which dims and blurs our vision along the path to wellness.

- **Pride.** Pride is one of the more subtle sins of persons. It is living egocentrically rather than theocentrically, i.e., putting self before God, acting as God. Pride isolates and brings loneliness which is one of the great stress causes.

- **Guilt.** To live in a sustained state of guilt is an insult to our Creator who has made us as his children and, as a loving father, wants us to sit on his lap folded in his forgiving arms feeling the joy of the warmth of his love. He does not want us to cower in the dark corner of shame and sorrow. A constant consciousness of guilt destroys the body, twists the mind, sears and severs the spirit.
- **Indifference.** Indifference is our not caring, sharing or daring. It is a limbo life, a no-man's land of doubt and darkness. A life of "status quoism" that blacks out the prism of light and colors that involvement and service to others bring.

## Some paths to a healthy spirit

The paths to wholeness of spirit are many. The following are significant.

- **Purgation.** Just as one's body and mind need to be cleansed, so does one's spirit. Confession, forgiveness, repentance, humility are ways in which one's spirit can be renewed and thereby may effectively cope with life's challenges. The mystical path to God always begins with purgation.
- **Service to others.** Too often we try to be holy persons just by holy words. Holy words without holy works lead to hollow words and hollow persons. Reaching out to help others in need is also reaching in and cultivating the seed of wholeness for ourselves.
- **Silence.** Silence and stillness allow the pool of our spirit to be calm and thereby perfectly reflect the light of God's love and will in our lives. Silence and stillness enable us to see more clearly to the depths of our own being and to caress gently the shores of other lives which our waters of life touch. In silence and stillness our lives become one-pointed and we gather direction, purpose and strength for the intentional living that brings peace and power.
- **Prayer and meditation.** These are spiritual "musts" on the path to wholeness. Each are outlets for the eternal yearning of the soul for God, the burning of the heart for God's love. Prayer and meditation are like catalysts that hasten the meeting of human and divine which bring fulfillment. They are journeys into joy.
- **Kinship with all.** To recognize and to realize in your being the unity of humanity is a big step toward total health. To recognize and realize the kinship with all of creation is a bigger and better step. When we exercise and encounter nature and the universe, we encounter ourselves. To believe that the universe is friendly is

most important in dealing with our stresses at all levels. A positive cosmology is necessary for an affirmative psychology.

- **Meaning and purpose.** To consciously affirm that your life has meaning and purpose is one of the most important spiritual dynamics for total health. He who has a **why** to live for can cope with any **how.** Meaning in life is not only the direction giver, but also a great source of power for healing.

- **Love.** The heart of power in the universe and of power within each of us is love. God is Love, we are made in God's image; therefore we **are** love. When we express love at its best we are being authentic, integrated, whole. In the final analysis, love is the great healer, the mainspring of our existence. Love is the source, the force and the course of our being. Whenever we are in great suffering and distress, ill of body or mind, we need always ask ourselves how we are expressing, or not expressing, love.

## More thoughts on Love

- The totality of love is not within the measure of the mind.
- That which wounds has no place in the Kingdom of Love.
- Love acts without thinking of love.
- Love cannot be based on demand.
- Love requires honesty and truth.
- Love seeks the good of the other, knowing the other may reject or strike back. Love does not allow the behavior of others to tell you how you feel.
- Your best love for another is your own inner transformation.
- The true self **is** love. Persons living from their authentic identities do not hurt each other and do not see another as a threat or rival.
- Love recognizes the spiritual identity of beings.
- Thinking about love is not the same as knowing love.

## Some guidelines for spiritual healing

- Realize that God's will and place for us is wholeness of body, mind, and spirit and that ultimately all healing is from God. A healer is the channel for the Creative Power — the gift bearer, not the gift Giver. The healer helps to create conditions (climate) for healing to take place and is often the catalyst for releasing the healing energies within the healee.

- Maintain singleness of purpose — i.e., to be a blessing to others. Develop the God-consciousness. Be aware of the God-presence in silent prayer and meditation.

- Exercise a strong, persistent faith in God's willingness and desire for wholeness. Hold fast to the truth that all things are possible with God.

- Love deeply. Love is the womb of wholeness; the cradle of creativity.

- Place the quest for healing in proper perspective. Healing is not an end in itself, but a process in the search for God. Thus, seek new learnings about your relationship to God. Don't lessen the lesson that comes.

- Be hopeful. Hope is the quiet sustaining power that teaches us each new day is new life.

- Be patient. God's delay is not God's denial.

- Be thankful. Thankfulness is pulsating to the heartbeat of God and brings healing vibrations. Live with an attitude of gratitude.

- Be expectant. Desire sincerely, but do not demand, that healing come about.

- Radiate joy. Joyfulness creates a climate for regeneration. A smile is a curve that makes many lives and conditions straight.

- Accentuate the positive. Realize the God and the good in the other. Focus on wholeness. Do not dwell on the illness in thought, word or deed.

- Accept a person where he or she is. Be kind, understanding and do not insist on rigid rules of conformity.

- Be humble. Shun spiritual pride and egotism. Personal gain and private glory are detriments.

- Be receptive and open. Dispel your doubts. Do not put a question mark where God puts an exclamation point.

- Relax and cultivate inner peace. Peace within facilitates harmony and healing without.

- Coordinate your healing efforts with others engaged in the healing arts. God's methodology, as well as His power, is unlimited.

- Be truthful. Seek to harmonize your thoughts, words and deeds so that in this perfect correspondence you are whole and a fit channel for healing.

- Abolish those desires and practices of the flesh that might block the healing power.

- Harbor no hatred, anger, resentment or fear. These create stress which builds resistance. If your heart is a volcano, the healing power cannot flow.

- Confess your sins to God, ask forgiveness and accept it. Also, forgive yourself; then renounce self condemnation, self-criticism, self-pity. Eradicate guilt feelings or any martyr complex.

# CHAPTER 16

# USE OF MEDITATION
# AND GUIDED IMAGERY IN
# HANDLING STRESS AND HEALING

There are three basic techniques you can learn very easily to help you develop your inner self to handle stress: *meditation, guided imagery and affirmation.* This chapter involves a description of the first two.

## Meditation, hypnosis, altered states of consciousness explained

Meditation is a technique whereby you voluntarily lower your brain wave frequencies to an altered state of consciouness while maintaining awareness. When you achieve the so-called meditative state your physical body is in a state of relaxation. Although your mind is also relaxed, it has reached a higher level of awareness, through which your spirit has achieved a higher state of consciousness.

While you are existing within this body, your mind is the key to entering higher levels of awareness and consciousness. When you are at these higher levels, you can achieve mastery over your body and emotions.

The important aspect of meditation is that it is voluntary and under your complete control. It is your decision and responsibility when and how you use it.

Hypnosis is similar to meditation in that it is also a technique which allows you to relax your physical body and reach an altered state of consciousness. When you practice self-hypnosis there is probably little difference. When you enter hypnosis through the guidance of a hypnotist, there is a certain amount of control and responsibility delegated to him. We promote meditation because this procedure emphasizes your responsibility. When you wish to increase your mind awareness, assuming responsibility puts your subsconscious on the alert that you wish to be master of this ship, that is, your message becomes evident on the conscious level. This is an important message to get through to your subconscious.

Altered states of consciousness are described in Chapter 7. Essentially, it is the state you are in when your brain is emitting ALPHA and THETA (and some DELTA) brain wave frequencies while you are awake and aware. Ordinarily, you experience these frequencies while you are asleep. Under those conditions I would not refer to your consciousness as being altered. However, when you are awake and experiencing these stronger, more energetic brain wave frequencies, you do achieve a heightened level of awareness. You have truly expanded your level of consciousness.

There are drugs that can also facilitate your entering altered states of consciousness, but with drugs you destroy your awareness, you mix up the bits of information within your bio-computer, you lose control and you may even destroy your ability to think. You may have bizarre experiences while under the influence of drugs, and the after effects may not only be confusing, but they may also be downright dangerous. Drugs are destructive to the mind. In my opinion, taking drugs is an undesirable way to self-realization.

## Active vs. passive meditation

Certain forms of meditation become mental exercises. Just as when you physically exercise, your muscles develop and maintain strength. Active meditation helps you develop your mental abilities and powers. The more you employ meditation, the better your mind power and the closer your goal become. On the other hand, when you stop meditating, your mental powers will deteriorate just as your muscles do when you stop exercising.

Active meditation is when you actively form images while you are still and quiet in the meditative state. It is an active, rather than a passive state. Transcendental meditation is a more passive approach to relaxation and some critics believe that, although TM can help you to relax your body, long term use of TM has a deleterious effect upon your mind. You may become almost mindless due to the fact that you empty your mind of thoughts. Again, for achieving physical relaxation TM may be OK, but to develop your mind, an indispensible part of your triune nature, TM may actually be counter productive.

Devote a portion of each day to active meditation. You eat every-day to sustain your body. Then you should also develop a program of feeding your mind daily. Employ active meditation to relax your body. This in itself will benefit many: you will achieve restful sleep; blood pressure will decrease to normal; you will improve your ability to cope with stressful situations; the need for tranquilizers and sleeping pills will disappear; and you will achieve inner peace.

Use guided meditation to create a positive constructive imagination and to develop and employ your powers of visualization. You may also use active meditation to develop and maintain your belief factor which will be discussed in more detail later. Use active meditation for general self-improvement purposes. It is the key technique that allows you to develop your mental powers to the fullest capacity.

It is safe and I know of no adverse side effects from its use.

## Is meditation harmful or evil?

Critics have stated that meditation is harmful, it is evil, it opens your mind to possession by demons. This is pure unadulterated garbage and reflects the thinking of some fanatics whose consciousness is not much higher than that of a rock! I will hasten, however, to add a warning. If you wish to meditate and you believe that when you do the demons will move in to possess your mind, **do not meditate.** It has nothing to do with demons. It has to do with your own belief.

Remember that when you reach the meditative state you are at stronger, more energetic brain wave levels and any picture that you create will be strongly impressed upon your subconscious mind. Do not impress negative pictures. There may be a built in fail-safe system within the mind, however. Some researchers believe that ordinarily if you try to create negative thoughts of anger, evil, hurt or harm, etc. you will pop out of your altered state of ALPHA and THETA. Whether this will stand up under scientific scrutiny, I do not know.

Nevertheless, it is still my opinion that you probably should not meditate if you have a strong negative belief about demons because these beliefs exist within the deeper recesses of your subconscious mind, and I do not know what might happen should these be released. I have not known of anyone harmed by meditation or who has experienced serious side effects from its use.

If you have strong negative beliefs, work on them first by using the technique of *affirmation*. Once you are convinced that you are ready to approach your subconscious with positive attitudes, then proceed.

## Guided imagery

Guided imagery is a technique whereby, while you are in the meditative state, you create and visualize with your imagination situations or conditions as you want them to be. Your subconscious self then brings them about.

This is actually how the mind functions normally. Although we are not usually aware of it, our hidden imagination feeds the subscious with ideas and pictures with which to function. Some conditions are good. Others are not so good. This is why we must be aware of what we are creating, so that the subconscious is at all times presented with ideas and pictures which we consciously desire.

Behind many of our illnesses are our negative creative imaginings. We allow our subconscious to be fed such things as fear, hatred, jealousy, etc. We have put these bits of information within the central communications center, the bio-computer. The subconscious is constantly drawing from the memory bank for the raw materials to create our every day reactions, feelings, and emotions.

We practice guided imagery during meditation because it is at the altered states of consciousness, at the slower, stronger brainwave frequencies of ALPHA and THETA, that we get the mental power to make stronger impressions on our brain cells enhancing the storage of these positive creative imaginings within our memory bank.

Guided imagery is the technique being used today by many to help people cure themselves of life threatening dis-eases, such as heart dis-ease and cancer. The Simontons (Cancer Counseling and Research Center, Fort Worth, Texas) are teaching terminal cancer patients guided imagery and many are curing themselves of disease at one time thought to be synonymous with death.

This is the same technique you can use to see yourself handling and mastering stressful situations. Dissolve stress in your imagination, in your mind. Watch it resolve and disappear in your BETA world reality.

When you wish to relax, enter the meditative state and picture yourself lying on the beach on a beautiful summer day or lying by a forest stream listening to the trickle of the brook with a slight breeze blowing through the trees overhead, or walking through a forest on a beautiful fall day with the sun shining through the trees with their reddish-golden leaves. Create any siutation that is peaceful to you and get absorbed by the beauty of this imaginary world you've created or which has appeared. Then experience your cells and mind relax. Experience your spirit leaping into another dimension.

When you wish to solve a particular health challenge, enter the meditative state and picture yourself well. You may require assistance at first to help you develop a creative imagery which will work for you with your particular health challenge. Do this daily or even several times daily if your particular health challenge is severe.

Use guided imagery to picture yourself handling life's situations as you would desire. Use it to improve your relationships with your fellow man. Practice being aware of your thoughts. Start to monitor them. Check out what the results may be and decide if you want that result. You have the reins. You can move or change the course according to your desires.

What you create in your imagination at these strong brainwave levels is what you will experience in life. What you can accomplish with guided imagery depends upon your effect and your belief.

## Some examples of healing

Meditation, guided imagery, and a positive belief system are powerful techniques to employ not only in coping and benefiting from stress but also in healing. We have known many individuals who naturally have mobilized their own innate healing abilities and powers to heal themselves of physical, mental, emotional, and spiritual illnesses. There have been others we have seen who have been taught how to activate their own healing potential. I am going to relate the story of two individuals who were able to heal themselves to demonstrate to the reader that there is more than just theory involved.

Christine F. is 24 years old and, since childhood, has been gifted with pronounced psychic abilities which she kept to herself most of her life for fear of being ridiculed. I had gotten to know her while she was student in the T-H-E-M-E (Total-Holistic-Enrichment through Meditative-Enlightenment) mental training program of our Center. She was aware of the extent of her psychic abilities and wished to develop them further.

She had a mole on her right cheek for as long as she could remember. All of a sudden it started to increase in size, and she considered going to a surgeon to have it removed. Her husband, who constantly ridiculed her psychic power, told her: "Why not forget about the surgeon and think the mole away?" Christine retorted: "O.K. I will." So she started to employ mental imagery to get rid of the growing mole. Within two days something started to happen to the mole: it got red and ugly looking and it started to exude fluid from the center. She was so excited, she called me to share her experience. I told her to come right over, that I would like to see what was happening.

When I examined the lesion I became somewhat concerned. It looked as though it were undergoing malignant (cancerous) changes. I did **not** indicate my concern to Christine at the time. I had no intention of laying my negativity on her. Instead, I asked her what **she** thought was going on. She responded that she was convinced that her body was rejecting the mole and that it was healing. I told her that was fantastic! I advised her to go home, keep up the good work, and continue her imagery. I asked her to let me examine her again in a week because I wanted to see how her healing was progressing.

One week later she had called me to tell me that it had healed completely and that there was nothing to see. I did see her several weeks afterwards and confirmed that fact that the mole was gone and there was no evidence that anything but normal skin had been there.

This is a good example of using imagination in a positive creative manner to cause a healing to occur. Christine combined this with her exercises of mental imagery (i.e. visualization) done at the stronger, more energetic brain wave meditative state. Let us all remember Christine's powerful belief: she was convinced all along that she could do it and she was able to envision in her mind the end result of a healed face. **It is truly this type of faith that heals.**

Mary S. had also taken our Center sponsored T-H-E-M-E mental training program upon the advice of a friend who had employed what he had learned to lower his blood pressure to normal levels without the use of anti-hypertensive drugs to which he reacted violently. Mary was very concerned about a condition she had for over 12 years: numbness and lack of significant sensation on one side of her right hand and involving two of her fingers. Twelve years previously she had undergone surgery in her neck and the surgeon informed her that she might experience temporary or permanent numbness and loss of sensation in part of her right hand.

There is a part of the seminar where we guide the participants into experiencing the altered THETA state of consciousness where many have experienced healings. Upon coming out of this state, Mary was visibly upset. She was crying. I asked her what was wrong. She told me that she felt nothing. Her hand had been numb for 12 years, and it really bothered her. Up until that time, I was unaware why Mary had come to the T-H-E-M-E classes. I asked her to tell me all about it, about what the doctors had done, what they told her, and what she experienced.

While talking to Mary, I had the feeling that she was a victim of her own belief in the doctor who performed the operation 12 years previously. I believed that Mary could be taught to use the same powerful belief system to her advantage. I explained to her that, when nerves are damaged, the portion of the nerve away from the damage site degenerates, but that regeneration does occur starting at the site of injury working down the nerve fibers to the most distal end. This regeneration, I told her, occurred at the rate of one millimeter (i.e. about $1/25$th of an inch) per day. Even if she were able to cure herself she had to allow time for the nerve to complete the regeneration process.

One month later she arrived at another seminar beaming from ear to ear and saying over and over that all normal feeling had returned to her hand that she was ever so grateful to me for curing her. I quickly corrected her by saying that I had done nothing. She had done it all. I was just fortunate to have been an instrument in her own healing.

I didn't want to bother Mary with the details, but I ask you to explain how she could have regenerated those nerves in such a short time — 30 days would have accounted for 30 mm of regeneration, that is about 1.2 inches. Mary's arm was about 30 inches long! The fact of the matter was that, if there had been damage to the nerve roots at the base of the neck, the nerves would have regenerated completely within two years after her operation, about 10 years before her taking the T-H-E-M-E seminar.

There are several things about which we are not sure. First, whether there was any damage to the nerve at all? In this case, Mary was expecting a loss of feeling sensation and her powerful belief brought it about. Second, there might have been damage and the regeneration which occured slowly, but surely was completed long ago. We do know that nerves are composed of thousands of microscopic fibers, and, when nerves repair themselves, regeneration of the proximal portion (the end closer to the spinal cord) may not occur down the same fiber route it had been connected to before. The brain, therefore, gets confused with the messages it receives after the nerve is repaired. A brain cell which was involved (trained) to control a small section of the skin is no longer receiving sensation from that same section but rather from another part of the skin. The brain must be re-taught. When Mary was expecting loss of sensation, this interfered with her ability to "reprogram" her brain cells.

There is one thing about which we are definitely sure. After years of no sensation in a portion of her right hand, Mary was able to completely restore the feeling to normal. She accomplished this through the use of her imagination, her powers of visualization, and her positive belief. It was her negative belief which had caused her to suffer all those years.

It is always heartwarming for me to see the faces of individuals when they eventually realize the true power they have within themselves. It is a source of great satisfaction to serve as an instrument in someone's healing. Mary did experience a true healing. This she accomplished herself. She had just been unaware before how to do it.

We can be either a victim of our own mind or our own liberator. Our education and way of living have not promoted the belief that we can control our bodies, minds, and spirit. When we begin to realize that we can, our education really begins, and our way of living changes. We begin to experience life with a new awareness.

## How to meditate and use guided imagery

The purpose of this book is not to teach you how to meditate and use guided imagery. These subjects would require another book and I am not yet convinced that it is easily learned from books. There are some things that are still best taught by demonstration. I believe that this is so with meditation. I do not mean to belittle books designed to teach you how to meditate. In my opinion, Larry LeShan's *How to Meditate* is an excellent and informative book. However, most individuals require serious personal instruction, especially if they wish to solve serious health or personal challenges.

You may at the outset be able to achieve the meditative state and know you are there. It is not difficult to meditate. All you really need to do is get to a quiet place in a relaxed position (preferably not lying down), close your eyes and tell yourself you are going to relax your whole body. As you do you tell yourself that you wish to reach a level of awareness whereby you can learn more about your inner mind self. There is nothing wrong in telling yourself what you hope to achieve. Talk to your subconscious. Tell it that you want to know. You have the right to know. Amazing what you will experience!

The challenge I found in meditation at first was not so much being able to achieve the meditative state but in knowing and being convinced that I was there. It had to do with my belief. **Belief factor is the power behind the workings of the mind.**

Another challenge is knowing what to do with the information coming to you in meditation. You can learn how to handle your thoughts, but it is best taught by someone with experience.

There are cassette tapes which can teach you how to meditate. Our Center has developed such tapes. They can help you arrive at ALPHA and THETA. Their use is not as good as individual instruction from someone competent in the field.

The purpose of this book is to expose you to the disciplines of meditation and guided imagery and, hopefully, to convince you of the usefulness of these in your future growth and development. You can begin to meditate on your own, and should you wish to develop this expertise further, you will be motivated to pursue it.

# CHAPTER 17

# USE OF AFFIRMATION IN HANDLING STRESS

## Affirmation to develop positive belief factor

Affirmation is a way of convincing your subconscious that you mean business. We have not stated much yet about *belief* other than having described your *belief factor* as one of the three keys to your mental power. We will now discuss the significance of *belief* in total holistic wellness.

Just how important is your belief system and your faith in the use of mind power? In my observations, I would conclude that without believing, the use of your imagination and power of visualization is almost useless! It is belief which supplies the real power behind the workings of the subconscious. We've seen this demonstrated over and over again. In fact, a weak imagination and a not too good visualization effort can oftentimes be offset by a powerful belief system. Many individuals have accomplished great physical and mental feats by knowing the power of belief and faith.

If you do not believe in the images you create and visualize (i.e., your imagery), your mind will not be totally convinced. If this be the case, your mind power will be wasted and ineffective. Your subconscious belief system is the important one, and this may be different from what you think you may believe consciously. Researchers have shown that health conditions are not related to what an individual states is his belief about his particular health challenge, but rather are directly related to his inner belief about it. In most cases an individual's inner belief is hidden from him. However, it can be and has been brought to light through meditation and self-hypnosis.

Our belief systems about dis-ease can prevent us from curing ourselves. We have been programmed to believe that cancer kills.

When you develop a cancer, your subconscious takes over and does the rest. It gathers these bits of information about cancer from your computer and says: "OK, I've-got-cancer; cancer-kills; therefore, my-body-must-die." You may want to consciously believe that you can cure yourself. What you need to do is develop the conscious mental strength to replace the negative bits of information with positive bits, and convince your subconscious that your new program is the one you desire to execute. If the power is there, you will succeed in curing yourself. If not, then you will die.

The fact is that during and since our very young development we've collected beliefs of the environment unconsciously and now find that we wish to change or redirect them. When you motivate yourself to replace the information you have to coincide with a change in attitude, the conscious mental strength comes forth to perform the desired result. The power is **always** present. It is how one **uses** it.

In chapter 7 we described the experiences of several cancer patients, two of whom died. Although both thought they wanted to live, they were unaware of what their subconscious believed. The third individual who lived took charge and directed his subconscious to carry out the process of eliminating his cancerous condition.

Remember that the inner subconscious is operating all the time, 24 hours a day. Your conscious mind is working only during those times that you are consciously thinking about it. Meditation guides you to experience greater awareness of where you are in your conscious thoughts. Also by meditation you may communicate directly with your subconscious mind-self and convince it to work for you. It takes imagination, creative thoughts, developing a positive belief system, and **work.**

Your belief system depends upon your faith which is a faculty of both your mind and spirit. I sincerely believe we are not primarily humans with a spirit, but rather we are primarily spirits, expressing through the human existence. At least, it is very helpful to think of us as such because we can use this belief to our advantage.

If we are primarily spirits then we are linked to the spirit world and we can call upon higher spiritual powers to give us strength to deal with human challenges.

Those who meditate a lot know of the existence of the spiritual world because they develop proficiency in communicating with it. Those of you who have not yet experienced this will have to use your faith to believe me. My advice is to work to develop a spiritual belief system. This does help in strengthening the spirit part of the body-mind-spirit triad. Eventually, with the three parts of your nature strong and active, you can go forward in your evolution.

## Affirmation as a key spiritual tool

Use affirmation to kindle spiritual fires. When someone asks me how I feel, I always answer quickly that I am *better, better and better.* I say this two or three times early in the morning and soon I am *better, better and better.* The first several times I say better, better and better it is an effort of my conscious mind. Soon it becomes a response from my inner subconscious self. Along with this quickening of my inner self, my spirit comes alive, I'm on a real emotional high, I become mentally more alert and my body is energized. Imagine all of this because I choose to consciously affirm that *I am better, better and better.*

We have put together a list of belief affirmations which we know will help you to develop a healthy inner belief system. These will prepare your mind to be receptive to higher forces and convince your inner self, so that your mind power can be effectively and efficiently utilized. You may develop your own personal belief affirmations, or if you wish, you may use the ones we present as a guide for preparing a set of affirmations of your own.

It would be better to state these affirmations while you are at the strong brain wave levels of meditation. So begin by closing your eyes and relaxing yourself. You may want to make a tape of the affirmations for yourself allowing enough time between affirmations to repeat them out loud or mentally to yourself.

As an alternative, after you reach the meditative state, open your eyes and read the belief affirmations, preferably out loud. If you read them out loud you will not only see the written affirmations, but also hear your own voice saying them, thus employing more than one of your senses to impress information upon your brain cells. Read slowly and contemplate for a few seconds the meaning and implications of each affirmation.

Another technique is to stand before a mirror and look at yourself while you state your affirmation. Although there is energy at the meditative state, there is also power in our physical sensing, especially with that of sight. See yourself stating the affirmations. Associate this with some positive body language. You will be amazed at how convincing this can be.

Before listing some sample affirmations, I must say a few words about God. I realize that there are many individuals who claim to be atheist and do not believe in God as such. Some may be agnostics who are not sure that there is a God. Others may believe in one God. And, there are probably as many conceptions about God as there are individual people. Some other references include Universal Mind, Infinite Source, Buddha, Christ Consciousness, and Life Force.

From a practical standpoint, I believe that if you were to believe that you have all the power within you to do whatever you desire to do, there may be times when you may actually doubt the existence of this power or your capacity to generate an unending supply of it. With your faith being shaken a bit, you may create a situation that causes further drain of your energy. Maintaining a belief in God as the Ultimate Source will cause your energy to be restored.

On one occasion I was spending four to six hours a day for about two weeks meditating and sending "healing energy" to a child dying of leukemia. After about one week I started to feel tired, and by the end of the second week I was literally coming apart at the seams. I had to stop my meditations of sending energy out and concentrate on building up my own energy status.

Several years later I asked Olga Worrall, the well known psychic healer, how she maintains her energy level and prevents energy drain during healing because there is a definite energy transfer that has been demonstrated from healer to subject. Olga's reply was that it was very simple. Just picture yourself as a channel through which God's infinite energy flows. Since you are but a conduit there is no energy drain from yourself. In fact, you become energized in the process.

The reason for telling the story is that it is to your advantage to develop a belief system which can work in your favor. If for no reason other than being practical, believe in God and watch the energy flow through you.

There was a young man once who was completing one of my *Coping with Stress* seminars. He came to me on the final seminar day and said: "On the first day of the course I was turned off by all that Spirit stuff you were talking about. But, you know, as the course went on and I meditated more, strange things began to happen to me. I found myself asking those dangerous questions: 'Who am I? , What am I?, Where am I going?.' I'm beginning to believe there is something out there bigger than all of us!" I nonchalantly replied with a twinkle in my eye and an air of *I told you so:* "My, isn't that interesting!"

On the first seminar day I ask all my students who claim not to believe in God to play a game with me and believe for a while. I have yet to encounter anyone who concluded the game was not worth playing. A point that we constantly are making throughout this book is to open your mind and increase your awareness of yourself and the world around you. There are two worlds out there: the material and the spirit worlds. The material world is a mere reflection of the spirit world and holistic awareness encompasses all three worlds, i.e. your body world, your mental world and your spirit world.

So as the saying goes: "Try it. You'll like it." Believe me when you begin to experience total (holistic) awareness you are going to really live.

## Belief Affirmations

Start by developing a series of **Belief Affirmations** that will establish for you a way of living. You may modify the affirmations we present below. Just make sure that you state them in a positive manner.

1. *I believe in the existence of God, a higher power, a force of love, that is eternal and puts meaning into our lives.*

2. *I believe that I have the mind-power to gain and maintain control over all of my life forces, both mind and body.*

3. *I believe that my own life force is an extension of the God force working within and through me.*

4. *Since the God force is all-powerful, then the life force within me is all powerful.*

5. *I believe that I can improve my life by improving my way of thinking.*

6. *I believe that I can acquire, experience, and maintain inner peace of mind.*

7. *I believe that life is worth living, that I am an instrument of the God force to do good.*

8. *I believe that love begins with me, that I can give love, accept love and share love.*

9. *I believe that I can conquer any bad habit detrimental to my mental and physical health and I can develop and maintain good health habits.*

10. *I believe that the God power within me can make my life more successful, and ever better, better and better.*

11. *I believe that I am master of my fate and that life is what I make it.*

I would like to call your attention to affirmations 1 to 4. Our subconscious mind is very logical. It is for this reason that we experience either wellness or dis-ease. Our bodies will respond very logically to what exists as mental thought programs in our subconscious mind. It is what I call "mental cause and physical effect." Observe the progression of logic from "I believe in the existence of God . . ." to "I believe that I have the mind power . . ." to "I believe that my own life force is an extension of the God force . . ." to "Since the God force is all-powerful, then the life force within me is all-powerful." It would appear that one follows very naturally and logically from the preceeding affirmation. Our subconscious mind can accept this logic.

Use your affirmations daily, twice daily if you are having difficulty establishing a positive uplifting attitude. If you should be doing your affirmations and you fail to do so, don't eat a meal until you do! Feeding your physical body should come after feeding the mind and soul. Obviously many modern day Americans fail to appreciate this!

You will definitely begin to experience benefits from your affirmations. Many students remark that it appears so simple. They also confirm that after they have tried affirming they begin to see their life change for the better. Remember that everyone is doing some form of affirming every day. The individual who says "I feel sick, I feel tired, my aching back," etc., is affirming, but he is being negative about it. So affirm only those things you wish to experience, not the ones you don't.

## Plans for Living

The purpose for the **Plans for Living** statements is to establish important mini-goals in your life. Take a few minutes and state these as you do your belief affirmations. I believe the **Plans for Living** are self-explanatory:

1. *I have developed a zest for life.*
2. *I devote a portion of each day to improving my health.*
3. *I devote a portion of each day to improving my mind.*
4. *I engage in some form of moderate daily exercise.*
5. *I go to bed at a reasonable hour each night so that I always have adequate rest and sleep.*
6. *I observe common sense rules about cleanliness and wear clothes that enhance my outer appearance.*
7. *I take time each day for some form of recreation that relaxes me.*
8. *I devote a portion of each day to meditate upon the God force that works within me.*
9. *I remain young in mind and spirit.*
10. *I am positive, and will associate and surround myself with positive uplifting people. Negative influences will not affect me.*
11. *I observe moderation in everything I do.*
12. *I practice controlled relaxation as a way of life.*
13. *I learn to grow wiser, and more loving and compassionate toward my fellow man.*

14. *I love life, I am glad to be alive, I have a will to live and I feel young.*

15. *Everyday in every way, I AM better, better and better.*

16. *I am master of my fate and captain of my soul.*

## Affirmations to control stress, nervous tension and chronic tiredness

1. *I am cultivating healthy living habits, such as eating a minimum amount of good healthy foods, exercising regularly, meditating frequently, and sleeping enough.*

2. *I am keeping my negative emotions under control. I am not going to get angry, be hateful or jealous, feel sorrow or nervousness, become irritable or have emotional outbursts.*

3. *I am loving, compassionate and kind to my fellow man.*

4. *In order to break tension I:*
   a. **Talk it out**
   b. **Take one thing at a time**
   c. **Get rid of my anger**
   d. **Cure my superman urge**
   e. **Take a positive step forward**
   f. **Do something for someone else**
   g. **Knock down the barbed wire fences.**

5. *I am learning to do everything in a relaxed way.*

6. *Relaxing allows me:*
   a. *To experience better physical health*
   b. *To get along better with people*
   c. *To think more clearly*
   d. *To be happier with my fellow man*
   e. *To be more tolerant*
   f. *To live longer.*

7. *I am conditioning my mind every morning to be positive throughout the day.*

8. *I am glad to be alive and life is a challenging adventure.*

9. *I am developing a sense of humor about life.*

## Affirmation to control anger and fear

1. *I am no longer afraid. Fear is a bad habit and I have the mind power to replace any bad habit with a good habit.*

2. *I am no longer angry. I will walk away from a person who is trying to provoke me into anger.*

3. *I have the self-confidence, understanding and wisdom to know that I have the power to think with my mind and not with my emotions.*

4. *Whenever possible I will try to laugh off a situation that is getting too serious by resorting to a sense of humor.*

5. *I am immune to people who try to upset me.*

6. *I am practicing tolerance and thinking and doing everything "the relaxed way."*

7. *I practice physical relaxation and meditation. When my body is relaxed my mind is relaxed and relaxation is the best way to prevent worry.*

8. *Meditation helps me to control the sick negative emotions of anger, hate, jealousy, fear and revenge.*

9. *I will always think pleasant thoughts about my fellow man and myself.*

10. *I love life and I am happy to live life now.*

11. *I like myself more because I am in control of my senses and appetites.*

## Affirmations to counteract depression and develop happy moods

1. *When people ask me how I feel, I will always answer: "I feel better, better and better all the time."*

2. *I will forget any misfortune that may have arisen in the past, from now on there are no problems. Instead, there are only challenges to stimulate my growth, development and understanding.*

3. *I welcome challenges as God's indication to me for my need to grow into new and higher understanding.*

4. *I get a feeling of well-being as I spice and flavor my life.*

5. *Since 95% of things we worry about never happen, I am not going to worry about anything.*

6. *I enjoy living today and I look forward to a better tomorrow.*

7. *I am keeping busy with work I enjoy.*

8. *I always think pleasant thoughts about my fellow man and myself. I love my fellow man, I love myself and I love God.*

9. *I love life and I am happy to live life now.*

10. *I will encourage and inspire others through my positive attitude to take steps toward improving their health.*

## Affirmations to achieve restful and happy sleep

1. *I am developing the habit of going to bed at approximately the same time each night.*

2. *I am correcting any uncomfortable situation that in the past contributed to my sleeping challenge.*

3. *I am relaxing my whole body and mind and tension will disappear from me. In fact, I will never be tense at any time.*

4. *I will always think pleasant thoughts about my fellow man and myself. I love my fellow man, I love myself, and I love God.*

5. *I feel sleepier and sleepier. I can sleep soundly any time I desire to do so.*

6. *There is no habit nor behavior stronger than the power of the mind. I have full control and complete dominion over my senses and faculties at all levels of my mind, including the outer conscious level. I am a superior human being, alert, healthy and positive.*

7. *I like myself more because I am in control of my senses and appetites.*

8. *I feel better, better and better and I am enjoying life more.*

9. *I will encourage and inspire others through my positive attitude to take steps toward improving their health.*

# CHAPTER 18

# THE CHALLENGE

## How to live a happy fulfilling life while benefiting from stress

**The cause of stress summarized.** I hope that by now you appreciate the fact that stress does **not** exist out there in the world waiting for you to come along. **It comes from within you.** It is your thinking that creates the stressful situation. It is the way you view life that makes stress in your life.

As mentioned in Chapter 1, *stress is a condition* **created within man by man himself** *of tension and upheaval brought about by his reaction to an internal or external situation.*

Do you feel intimidated by anyone? Your boss, husband or wife? How about your children? An individual intimidates you because you choose to view him or her that way, not necessarily because he or she has fearful traits. If you judge others as being fearful, they will be fearful to you. If you choose to view them as loving brothers or sisters, they will be lovable to you.

We should be thankful that we are responsible for the stress, anxieties, fear and depression because if we created these things in our lives we can "de-create" them. Tension is an unnatural experience. Lower animal forms do not appear to experience internal strife, except where it is a protective instinctive device warning against danger necessary for survival.

Also in Chapter 1, some of the inner sources of stress are described: anger, fear, impatience, rigidity, perfectionism, inability to relax, excessive competition, lack of humor and enthusiasm, chronic worrying and mental depression.

It has been shown that you can relax your negative emotions away and that you can substitute the energizing and uplifting positive emotions of love, tolerance and cheerfulness. Become aware of the reasons behind your anger and hatreds. Know that you can learn and master love and tolerance. This will help you to achieve a permanently healthy mind, soul, and body.

The positive emotions of love, tolerance, being cooperative and cheerful are uplifting and self-energizing and, if practiced regularly, can eventually replace the undesirable emotions.

If you're plagued by intolerance, try to develop love and tolerance of others by being an observer of them. In time, inner peace and harmony will be your reward.

If you're rigid, learn to be flexible. Allow others the right to express their personalities according to their imagination and understanding. There are many ways of doing things, not just your way. Be flexible and learn what the Universe has to offer.

If you're a perfectionist, do not be afraid of apparent failure for it may be good for you to fail. It may encourage you to create another way, and you may be the Universe's instrument for great discovery.

If you're uptight, learn to relax your body and mind. Put aside a portion of time each day and devote this to yourself. Regular practice pays regular dividends.

If you lack humor, learn to laugh and feel excitement. Believe me you will feel better.

Analyze the causes of your unhappiness and depression. You may be too sensitive to criticism; feel hurt whenever you feel rejected; dislike your physical appearance, being too fat, too thin, unattractive, etc.; become irritable when tired; be shy around people; lack self-confidence and worry about everything; feel sorry for yourself and seek sympathy from family and friends; be too suspicious about people's motives; get quickly discouraged; be immature about accepting ordinary responsibilities; have undue resentment of others and be disillusioned by people; be living in the past and be pessimistic about the future; be obsessed with the thought of being a failure and a victim of hard luck; be a health-neurotic and indulge in excessive health-complaining; or be obsessed by a particular health condition such as impotence, menopause, etc.

Remember that obsession can result in an ever increasing circle of aggravation. Any physical condition is capable of influencing the mind and the mind in turn can add fuel to the fire leading to further depression. Being obsessed with the idea that you are depressed further adds to your depression. If you label yourself as being "depressed" you merely reinforce this negative situation of suggestion and your mind will begin to believe it. If you have any of the traits that lead to depression, develop a list of affirmations to counteract the negative tendency. Affirm that: **There is no habit nor behavior stronger than the power of my mind. I have full control and complete dominion over my senses and faculties at all levels of my**

**mind, including the outer conscious level. I am a superior human being, alert, healthy and positive.**

Chapter 2 describes how we got the way we are and why we do the things we do. We are indeed victims of our childhood background and conditioning (programming), but, we must not cop out here. We don't have to be victims of our past. We don't have to be imprisoned by a negative subconscious. We must believe that we are truly spiritual beings undergoing a human experience. As spiritual beings, our potential is infinite.

As described in Chapter 3, you must determine your goals in life. Write them out and contemplate them daily. Always maintain faith in your God-given spiritual power for the strength to persevere.

In Chapter 4, you were taught how to achieve your goals holistically. We are composed of body, mind, and spirit, and when we unify these three aspects of our being we will function as a "whole" person. This can be done.

Attempt to appreciate the destructive nature of unresolved stress. Chapter 5 describes how nervous tension, the worry habit, chronic tiredness, emotional instability, mental depression, despair and insomnia can result when stress is allowed to exert a negative influence. Physical dis-eases can become manifest as a result: chronic pain, headaches, heart dis-ease, ulcers, ulcerative colitis, obesity, arthritis, insomnia, multiple sclerosis and cancer, to list a few. Finally, spiritual bankruptcy ensues and the will-to-live is affected.

Stress can be an useful encounter (Chapter 6). Use stress to learn about yourself. Before you can carry out any program of self-help or self-health you must first develop an increasing awareness about the factors which influence your thinking and know whether you are an actor or a reactor in life's situation. Assume the responsibility for your thinking and doing. Affirm: **I am responsible for my way of thinking. I am responsible for my way of acting. I will make whatever changes are necessary so that I become a positive thinking individual.**

The key to handle stress is in your mind. Chapter 7, the most important chapter in the book, describes the constructive use of your mind in coping with stress. Be aware of the difference between your brain and mind and how your conscious and subconscious minds operate. The three keys to mind power (awareness) are described: the effective use of your mind depends upon the proper and constructive use of your imagination, the development and use of your powers of visualization, and the degree to which you believe, i.e., your belief factor.

Once you recognize the fact that you are thinking and acting negatively you are then ready to do something about it. By practicing how to reject negativity you will gradually create positive situations in your life. Chapter 7 describes how you can do this. Learn how to set goals in your life. Then, keep your eyes on your goal and power your drive at your full potential of creative energy. You are then ready to experience life as it is intended and as you'd like it: beautiful, joyful, and full of love.

Chapter 8 describes how you can use stress as a positive and beneficial force in your life. You learn how to develop a positive attitude about stress so that you can use the challenges in your life for your own physical, mental, emotional and spiritual growth and well being. Learn how to take disappointments and use these for positive growth and development. There are infinite opportunities around us waiting for a creative being to develop. Learn to be that creative being.

Discover the harm of tranquilizers, uppers and downers, pep pills, sleeping pills, etc. Chapter 9 describes the destructive nature of these drugs which interfere with body chemistry and actually prevent you from activating and mobilizing healing chemicals produced by your own body. Tranquilizers, sedatives, and narcotic drugs have many adverse side-reactions which can be more devastating than the dis-ease being treated. Know about and avoid the trap of drug addiction. Learn about some exciting information from mind and brain research: how our right and left sides of the brain function. Use the information in Chapter 7 to develop both sides of your brain and mind.

Chapter 10 tells how diet affects stress. The food you eat affects not only your physical health but also your mental, emotional, and even your spiritual. The modern American diet is probably the worst diet ever devised. Be aware of highly processed foods which have been so altered that they are devoid of natural vitamins and other essential micronutrients. Chemicals in the form of preservatives and colorings further add poisons to our food. Toxic foods are described: refined sugar, white flour, polished rice, red meat, butter and other animal fats, coffee and tea, etc. Appreciate the fact that our mind and spirit depend upon our bodies for expression here on earth. The quality of our existence is directly dependent upon our physical health, and our physical well being is dependent upon our diet. A balanced natural diet is described so that you can begin to make changes in your way of eating to improve the quality of your life.

Exercise is also very important. Chapter 11 describes how physical exercise affects our ability to handle stress. Because physical exercise affects our metabolism, we must consider an integrated program of exercise and diet to maintain our physical bodies at top strength and efficiency. Aerobic and anaerobic forms of exercise are discussed and an aerobic exercise formula is given.

Physical dis-ease interferes with your coping ability. Chapter 13 describes how some physical dis-ease states not only cause but also result from stress. All physical dis-eases result in drainage of energy, the same energy an individual needs to employ in coping. Learn to regenerate your intrinsic energy stores and begin to experience the fullness of life maintaining that fantastic state of physical, mental, emotional, and spiritual wellness which is our destiny.

Chapter 14 shows how mental and emotional attitude affects your coping ability. The mind is where it's at! You tend to blame others for the bad that happens to you, when, in reality you cause both the good and the bad in your life. You must learn to create within your own mind positive images of what you want to experience. You can learn how to do this. When you do, you can begin to live life more abundantly.

Spiritual health is a key aspect of total (holistic) wellness. Chapter 15 describes how your spiritual health affects the overall state of well-being and your ability to cope. Although spirit is more difficult to define, it is nevertheless an important part of man's triune nature together with body and mind. The key to a healthy spirit is love. Hate destroys the spirit faster than anything else. You **must** learn to practice love everyday in your life to feed the spirit just as you must eat and exercise daily to keep the body healthy.

Chapters 15 and 16 delineate the three basic techniques you can use to handle stress, namely affirmation, meditation, and guided imagery. Affirmation helps you to develop a positive belief factor. Sample affirmations are listed to help you understand and handle stress, nervous tension and chronic tiredness, control anger and fear, eliminate depression and develop happy moods, and achieve restful and happy sleep.

Meditation is the key technique to achieve altered states of consciousness. At these states you are emloying stronger, more energetic mental energy to achieve contact with your subconscious mind. In addition, you can learn how to use this energy to make those changes you wish to make in your life and to cope with stress. We do have the power within ourselves to handle all of life's situations as they arise. We just have to learn how to mobilize our inner strength to do it.

Guided imagery is the technique of creating mental pictures of our goals. These pictorial goals are energized by the energy derived from meditation. We can experience whatever we wish to experience, provided we know what it is we want in our lives.

## Are there any quick practical solutions?

Our modern fast-paced life style is affecting many individuals in their thinking and acting. There is a type of arrogance which affects many. For instance, some individuals insist on abusing their physical bodies by eating too much and the wrong foods, lack of exercise, too little rest, etc. Others abuse their minds and spirit by their thinking and their way of living. When they get sick, they scurry to their physician or priest expecting a pill or a prayer to get them back into shape. Then, when they feel well, again, they are back living the same life, continuing to abuse their bodies, minds, and/or spirit once again. This cycle is repeated many times over the years. Eventually, the body/mind/spirit decides it isn't going to take it any more. Physical, mental, and emotional dis-eases ensue.

Are there any quick practical solutions? Yes, there are many, and no, there are none! There are many specific suggestions and much advice we could give to help you resolve or lessen the impact of a particular stressful event. We have made many throughout this book. But, unless, you **sincerely** desire to re-orientate your thinking and way of living, and establish a healthy life style, your stresses and challenges will recur.

Define your primary, secondary, and tertiary goals in life. Write them down and refine them as time goes on. Design your own program of self-improvement and self-health. Effectively utilize your time and apply the rules of *Scientific Prayer* for achieving your goals.

## Scientific Prayer

Scientific prayer is based upon using your Imagination, Powers of Visualization, and Belief Factor constructively towards accomplishing a specific goal. The following 12 **Rules of Scientific Praying** should be applied to fulfill the promise: "Go within to your inner closet and pray in secret and all things will be added to you according to your faith."

1. **ADJUST YOUR SELF IMAGE** to accept love, success, whatever you desire.
2. **BE SPECIFIC** in what you desire to be, have or do. Crystallize your thinking: determine what specific goal you want to achieve. Then dedicate yourself to attaining it with unswerving singleness of purpose, the energetic zeal of a true believer and crusader.
3. **CREATE A BURNING DESIRE** so strong that you can taste it. A burning desire is the greatest motivator of every human action. The desire for success implants "success consciousness" which, in turn, creates a vigorous and ever-increasing "habit of success."
4. **WRITE DOWN YOUR NEW DREAM.** You should put it in writing. This crystallizes your thought in reality.

5. **DEVELOP A PLAN** for achieving your goal. Plan your progress carefully: hour-by-hour, day-by-day, month-by-month. Organized activity and maintained enthusiasm are the well-springs of your power.

6. **GIVE IT A TIME,** an exact date for the happening. This focuses the time dimension into your dream picture, so that you need not wait an infinity for your answer.

7. **BLESS IT.** Accept your new life condition only if all concerned are blessed; as the Huna philosophy states; "for the good of all concerned, no hurt, no harm to anyone."

8. **VISUALIZE IT.** In your mind's eye, imagine and see things as you would have them instead of as they are.

9. **CUT THE CORD AND LET NATURE DO IT.** After visualizing your dream 10-15 minutes once or twice daily, let the thought go and let Nature (Universal Consciousness) bring it about.

10. **BUILD YOUR FAITH.** Belief is what creates reality. Eliminate all doubt. Be intense (not tense) and energize your new creation into reality. Relax your mind. Pray believing you have already received. Develop supreme confidence in yourself and your own abilities. Enter every activity without giving mental recognition to the possibility of defeat. Concentrate on your strengths, instead of your weaknesses — on your powers, instead of your challenges.

11. **TAKE THE FIRST STEP** toward making your dream a reality. "Faith without works is dead." Develop a dogged determination to follow through on your plan, regardless of obstacles, criticism or circumstances or what other people say, think or do. Construct your determination with sustained effort, controlled attention, and concentrated energy. Opportunities never come to those who wait. They are captured by those who dare to attack and do.

12. **TELL NO ONE.** Preserve silence. Do not dissipate your energy by letting another's negative thinking influence you. You may share your dream **after** it becomes a conscious reality.

## Summary

The holistic view is that man has a triune nature of body, mind and spirit. These three aspects must be integrated to function in harmony so that man functions as one — as a whole being. Stress reflects disharmony in our lives. Rather than allowing stress to be a disruptive and destructive force, we can, instead, use it to learn about ourselves. We can find out who we are and why we act the way we do. We can increase our awareness of both our inner self and the worlds around us. We can make whatever changes are necessary to grow and develop in ways which allow our spirit to evolve to higher levels of consciousness. We can achieve all of these goals.

This book should serve to begin to open your eyes, especially your spiritual eyes, to your infinite capabilities. As mentioned throughout this book your capacity to enjoy physical, mental, emotional, and spiritual health is but an attitude away — **your** attitude!

THE BEGINNING

# POSTSCRIPT

Although we believe that your health is your responsibility, we do not intend to suggest that the physician and other health professionals have no role. Some individuals may tend to follow the advice in this book blindly. If you believe or would like to believe in the principles we describe then by all means catch the ball and run with it. If you have a serious disease, seek out the assistance and guidance of a physician to help you put into practice what you wish to do. For instance, although the advice on aerobic exercise (Chapter 11) is sound and safe, if you have serious heart disease, we would recommend that you ask your physician to assist you in determining what might be the safe limits for you as you build up your exercise program. If your particular physician is closed to "new ideas," wants to do it his way, and refuses to accept your role in your own healing, then seek out another physician who is receptive. There are many health professionals who can and will support you in your holistic health endeavors.

# OTHER BOOKS
# BY THE AUTHORS

*(How To Obtain Them)*

*Awaken The Genius In Your Child* by Nicola M. Tauraso and L. Richard Batzler, 1980, Hidden Valley Press, $6.95.

*Manual of Positive Attitude Training Techniques for Children and Young Adults* by Nicola M. Tauraso and L. Richard Batzler, 1981, Hidden Valley Press, $15.00 (Manual contains 2 cassette tapes).

*Recommendations for Healthful Living — An Holistic Approach*, a health program of The GOTACH Center For Health, 1981, Hidden Valley Press, $5.95.

These books can be purchased by sending the appropriate fee to Hidden Valley Press, 7051 Poole Jones Road, Frederick, Maryland 21701.

All proceeds (royalties) derived from the sale of these publications are donated to The GOTACH Center For Health for building a residential/camp facility dedicated to and to be used by children, to teach and help them "awaken" their "genius," and for use by children and adults who desire to explore creative alternatives of healing.